32 COUNTIES

Storm over The Burren, Co. Clare

32 COUNTIES

Photographs of Ireland by Donovan Wylie
with new writing by thirty-two Irish writers

Secker & Warburg

For my grandmother Elizabeth Winifred McHenry

I left school at sixteen with two O-levels: Art and Photography; a year later I left my home in Belfast and walked into Ireland. I had many preconceptions about the island before I left, all of which were shattered as I travelled from county to county. The people I met while hitch-hiking round the country were all as various as the classes, cultures and religions that contain them. The poverty and the conflict are man-made, the land is not; and that is what remains. At times, when I was sitting on a mountainside in Connemara or Kerry, the complications of life on this island seemed reduced, once again, to enormous simplicity.

Donovan Wylie

From the Great Sugar Loaf Mountain, Co. Wicklow

COUNTY WICKLOW

Aidan Mathews

Question: You admit that you've been asked to write an essay about Wicklow?

Reply: Quite. Yet perhaps I should answer more accurately by using an Irish phrase instead of an English adverb. Perhaps I should answer: yes and no. Perhaps I should answer: more or less. Because, yes, I have been asked to write an essay, but only insofar as the very word 'essay' can remember and retrieve its original intention in French.

Question: And what's that? I would add that I'm asking simply and solely for rhetorical reasons.

Reply: An essay's only an attempt. In my own case, it's an attempt to interpret the ways in which Wicklow has been a presence in my past existence and an absence in my present life.

Question: You mean you've moved? You mean you're not living in Wicklow any more?

Reply: I never did live in Wicklow. Wicklow was for holidays and Holy Days; it was a plus, a surplus.

Question: This is awful. In fact, it's appalling. Don't you understand what this book is about? It's about thirty-two writers coming to grips with their own genesis. It's about men and women all over the country – a legion of literary luminaries and lightweights – finally facing up to those morose, metaphysical landscapes we call Roscommon, Donegal, or whatever. It's about the dialectical relationship between creativity and procreativity. For Christ's sake, even the photographs are in black and white. And you talk to me about holidays, about Sunday outings in the family car. I suppose you're going to tell me it was a banjaxed Beetle with a wobbly skeleton in the back window, or maybe a nodding poodle. I mean, this whole project is about cradles of consciousness, not about getting carsick.

Reply: I think the car was a Chevrolet. I seem to remember running-boards and lots of chrome ashtrays. Once it was lashing rain and we gave a lift to an old farmer up near Rathdrum. But the smell of him was so bad, the smell of not washing, that we had to open the windows. And I was so ashamed. Because I think he knew, because I know he knew. He got out early, while it was still raining. Even though he had no overcoat. And I went back to my sister's copy of the *Bunty*, and I read it all except the last page where she'd cut out all the paper skirts and swim-suits. But the next day, when my father drove me to the dentist's to have an abscess drained, the upholstery still smelled of the old man.

Question: I'm genuflecting. Believe me, I'm overcome by your subtlety and your sensitivity. So even at eight you died for the dispossessed. Maybe you were the first liberation theologian out of Donnybrook, Dublin 4. But that's not the point. The point

2 A day spent on Bray Head, Co. Wicklow

3 Wilderness deep in the Wicklow Mountains

is Wicklow. A coastal county south of the capital. A place where people are born and buried, where they grow up and grow old amid — or is it amidst, I never know which — scenes of striking sublimity, geological grandeur, Helvetian altitudes. I don't mean to hit the high C, but I am under pressure. I thought your typewriter stank of turf-smoke; now you tell me you went to Wicklow when the water in the pool had to be changed.

Reply: A place can be a home without being a house, just as a space can be a house without being a home. Where you sleep is less important than where you wake and walk, and Wicklow woke me. It was a personal domain by the time I was old enough to be afraid of the dark; an inner domicile by the time I was old enough to be more afraid of the light. So, if I didn't live in it, I lived out of it. And I still do.

Question: How's that?

Reply: I live on the brink of two counties, between Dublin and Wicklow. I like to think that the line of division passes through my house, between the tumble-drier and the Penguin Classics, or, if you lift it to the second level, straight down the middle of the marital bed and on into my study where, in fully five years, I've written only one thing, and that was a cheque.

Question: And where is the boundary between city and country, between concrete and clover?

Reply: First there's a field beside us, with a herd of cows in it. They kept us awake with their mooing a while back, because whoever milks them had forgotten to do it that day. My wife had been breast-feeding a short time before, and I had to stop her going out in her dressing-gown with a pail to fetch help. Anyhow, the factory that makes microchips is in the next field, and then there's a pitch-and-putt course that went bust. Beyond that there's the main road where the child was killed. Wicklow begins and ends, you see, in such inordinate particulars.

Question: So the suggestive symbolism of your living by design and not by default on the very faultline between two counties both reflects and reveals a double inheritance. But is that inheritance a divided one, and, if so, is it also divisive?

Reply: Listen. About the only thing an Irishman is able to inherit, apart from the shape of his mouth or the width of his shoulder-blades, is the state of divisiveness — so that's a silly question. The reason I live where I do is because my wife couldn't get a higher mortgage. But it's fine, it suits me. Besides, I like intersections. I like junctions. Intersections and junctions are invigorating. They train you to look left and right all the time. That way, you don't decay into too much attitudinising. You don't become ideological, which is a long Graeco-Roman word for dead. Instead, you live, move, and have your being in beginnings and ends. What you avoid is middles. Middles defeat most of us. But where I live is all openings and closings: blackberry ditches, dormitory suburbs, satellite dishes among pink fuchsia, double-decker buses skinning the spring growth on a copper beech tree that was strong and stately before Edison invented the light bulb, or a barrister shaving gingerly around a pimple on his throat while two small children and a collie shift sheep from the centre of the back road into town.

Question: That's a very beautiful image. I don't mean to interrupt the process of insight, but I would like to call attention to the barrister and the sheep. Sensitive readers will want to pause at that point. Because there you're condemning the whole process of conurbation, the way the city metastasises into the country, spreading like secondaries through hill and hedgerow. I remember where the salmon used to leap down in that place where I got the puncture, and now the only smell of salmon you'll come across in those parts is in a dish of quiche, though it's terribly expensive ever since it got that write-up in the paper. That's conurbation in a nutshell, of course.

Reply: I'm not talking about conurbation. I'm talking about incongruity. I'm talking about living in an atmosphere which mixes foxgloves and carbon monoxide. Even the names announce and pronounce the differences. Dublin is plump and tubby, it smells like the inside of a bowler hat, it smells of Brylcreem and cheroots; but the word Wicklow is like the sheen off brambles when the rain stops, and you come out from under the bare tree where you were sheltering, and you only realise how cold your hands are when you cup them to light a cigarette and the flame from the last pub match in the packet doesn't scorch your fingers. But the mountains around you are gleaming like glasshouses as the sun comes out again, and the woman you're with has tucked up the sleeve of her anorak and you can see the pinch-marks on her wrist where her budgie perched that morning.

Question: And that's Wicklow?

Reply: Yes. That's Wicklow. My Wicklow.

Question: A little bell in a birdcage, an addiction to nicotine, and a bit of fumbling, foreplay even, under a dead elm during a downpour. That's it?

Reply: It was enough at the time. It was more than enough. She warmed my hands between her legs, and sang the first few lines of a song by Cat Stevens; but she couldn't remember the second verse.

Question: Wait. Wait a moment. This book might sit on coffee-tables, in convent parlours. In all probability your own parents will end up with your free copy as a Christmas present. Have you no sense? Have you no shame? Warming your hands and whatever.

Reply: She was wearing trousers at the time. With a ski-school badge sewn on the left practice slope.

Question: She could have been wearing chain-mail for all I care. The question is, where does it lead us? And where does it leave us? It leaves us nowhere. It's a complete cul-de-sac.

Reply: And you want a Roman road, a royal route, the straight line of least resistance. But the memory doesn't move from A to Z, as the crow flies; it moves from Alpha to Omega, from shoehorns to a solar eclipse, as the wind wills. And you must learn to let it blow the tie over your shoulder, the crease out of your hair. You must learn to think in Greek and not in English. Here there is neither highway nor byway. There is only a right of way, trampled grass springing back up, a trail strewn with bubble gum and eucalyptus leaves. Up in the branches, birdsong.

Question: The budgie. It got out.

Reply: Can you hear something? Can you overhear something?

Question: No, I can't. You want me to feel bad about that?

Reply: Breathing through his mouth in bursts. The tips of his fingers on the handlebars are black with oil from the chain.

Question: Who?

Reply: That's John Millington Synge with a copy of *Thus Spake Zarathustra* in the basket of his bicycle as he pedals on solid rubber tyres toward a picnic spot in the pine forest; and the woman he's waving to, the woman in flared denims and a cheesecloth blouse, is on day-release from a private clinic in Dublin. She's meant to be picking wild flowers for tomorrow's class in Occupational Therapy, but she can't stop thinking about two years before when her second toddler touched the high-voltage cable, and white smoke like the smoke in churches poured from his *Star Trek* sneakers.

Question: And she can't stop thinking about that?

Reply: It's even more complex. She simply can't stop thinking. No more than the rest of us. Because always to be thinking is what makes us human. The daylight calls us to it, and the darkness too. Sleep, when it comes, is a consolation prize. But there are others.

Question: Such as?

Reply: Waking.

Question: And?

Reply: Snow, seedless grapes, the smell of a child in her sleep-suit, Palestrina's *Mass* for Pope Marcellus II, and the latest ad for Wrangler's where a foxy motor-cycle cop makes her toyboy spread-eagle himself while she frisks him for a hidden weapon.

Question: So there's a brighter side?

Reply: So bright it makes your eyes water when you look at it.

Question: Tell us.

Reply: There's Charles Stewart Parnell in the master bedroom of the house in Avondale, watching the mirror in amusement as Katherine O'Shea darkens the grey in his beard with her eye-liner; and the couple from Cabra filing along the cordon a century later while the guide recites the details of their death and downfall don't give a damn because today was day fourteen in her cycle, and so they took the phone off the hook and they made love, and maybe this time they'll have a baby. Saul would be a lovely name for a boy, and a lovely name for a girl would be Juliet.

Question: You wouldn't have a Saul in Cabra. Isn't Cabra working-class?

Reply: I've no idea. I only chose it because it alliterated with couple and cordon.

Question: Well, at least it was a nice picture. You know, if you put your mind to it, you could paint some lovely pictures.

Reply: I'm not a painter.

Question: But you know what I mean. What you go in for is the grisly business, a sort of shalom to the gallows. Every sentence you write lets the draught in. It's all knees knocking, and no knees up. But you mustn't scapegoat Wicklow. Wicklow is mild, Wicklow is mellow. They shot *Barry Lyndon* there, for God's sake. In the chocolate-boxy parts, anyhow. Waterfalls and wilderness. They have this way of rubbing out the telegraph poles when they do the developing.

Reply: Glencree is a wilderness, and a waste land too. I can see it, I can see the old reformatory.

Question: Industrial school.

Reply: Borstal. When I was a child, I was terrified of being sent to Borstal. Sometimes my parents threatened me with an Irish-speaking school. That was worse.

Question: Glencree's a pretty place, a picnic spot. Ministers drive down there in state cars to open Arts events at the Craft centre.

Reply: I can see a whole family stepping out of a Volkswagen in the days before seat-belts. The mother looks like Charles II without the moustache, but she's not posing for a portrait. Her face is vexed.

Question: Feminine timidity. And trepidation. Industrial schools can be disconcerting if you come from a culture where every child has his own initialled napkin-ring.

Reply: She's vexed because the colour ran on a cerise slip in the washing-machine that morning, and she's a shirt short for the three boys tomorrow. Her elderly father's pissed off as well: he's forgotten to take the daily aspirin that the doctor had told him would thin his blood, and he always takes it at twelve noon exactly. So he vents his tension by voicing the view that the prison should open its doors again to all the tykes and the tearaways and the law lecturer from the university who has sideburns and talks about underprivilege.

Question: Sound man.

Reply: Children are watching from the window. Three children.

Question: What children?

Reply: Reformatory kids. Boys from the college of chronic neglect. Each of them at their full height a full foot shorter than my four brothers. They're wearing green cardigans that a local Protestant never stops knitting, so it must be winter, the acoustic of frost. The one with the chilblain on his thumb, he'll be an ice-cream man in Coventry, arriving home from *Blazing Saddles* late on a Wednesday evening to discover that his daughter Naoise is a case of cot death at seven months.

Question: Naoise isn't a girl's name. It's a boy's name.

Reply: He didn't know that. And the curate at the christening didn't care. The day before he'd baptised an Ivory, and she was a black from Burundi.

Question: But you told me the place was closed. Glencree, I mean.

Reply: What has happened in time must happen in eternity. That's why the fellow in front of Chilblains will be back again when he's thirty-two, kicking a football at the painted goalposts, just as he did in the sleet and sunshine of a present past.

Question: But it isn't fair.

Reply: No, it isn't fair. It's beautiful.

Question: I meant the way you go on about Wicklow. You make it sound like a war-cemetery. What about the donkey rides in Greystones, and your mother walking beside you, trying to get the old Kodak camera to work? Or the Djouce woods? What about up in the Djouce woods, collecting pine-cones for the fireplace in your front room? They went up like Molotov cocktails, those pine-cones did. They were as good as grenades.

Reply: When they shot the Auxiliary officer, that time in 1920, it was up in the Djouce woods. The fellow who pulled the trigger came up along the side of the car while the Englishman's fiancée was trying to remove an eyelash from his eye with the edge of a handkerchief she'd first softened in soda-water. She told them after the post-mortem how the killer had looked at her and said, 'I'm very sorry about this, ma'am,' and how she'd never thought that a murderer would be wearing bicycle-clips.

Question: When you're in a state of shock, you're not thinking clearly. It's all a blur.

Reply: If that's so, there are many of us in a state of shock from rocking-horse to rocking-chair, from nappy rashes to scattered ashes.

9 Picnic, Bray, Co. Wicklow

Question: There you go again. The same sad, stricken note. It's all cello and no cha-cha. What you need is more Motown and less metaphysics. Now the next time you go to the Djouce woods, disabuse yourself of assassins with manners. Take a Walkman. Look out over the Powerscourt estate at the waterfall waterfalling down. It's so beautiful. You could make a television commercial there.

Reply: When I want to look at landscapes, I buy postcards. That way, I get a private viewing. Besides, copies are usually an improvement on originals.

Question: Are you saying that somewhere like the Djouce woods will only ever be a morgue that runs red with the blood of a quite inconspicuous homicide which will never be forgotten because it was never remembered in the first place? Are you saying that?

Reply: The cars came in convoy, one behind the other. They stopped at the same spot. Everybody got out.

Question: Don't tell me there was a massacre at the Djouce woods. I hit a sheep there once, but I couldn't stop or go back. My reverse gear was broken. Left a bloody big dent in my bumper too. You wouldn't think a sheep could do that much damage. Thanks be to Christ it wasn't a cow.

Reply: It was a family, an extended family, cousins, aunts and in-laws. They brought flasks and six-packs and sandwiches with the crusts on. They sat at a Forest Trail picnic-table, and turned on the transistor and listened to the shipping forecast, and the young mother went in among the trees to breast-feed her baby. But the boy-friend and his girl-friend had found a clearing in the conifers, and they lay down there. Her mouth smelled of yoghurt and Miwadi. There were so many buttons on his shirt, and she said: let me. And all over the world there were couples lying down, lying down in hotel suites and hillside shacks, in the green venue of their unison, men and women with the faces of children, out of a desire that was like grief, out of a need that was like anguish, under the dogged joy of the sun.

Question: I hope she was on the pill. That's all I say. The poetry turns to prose pretty fast if the oestrogen levels aren't right.

Reply: Afterwards –

Question: Hold it. Hold it right there. You haven't told us what happened yet. First you set a scene, then you strike the set. You're all prologue and epilogue. The middle's misty. What happens there? What happens in the meantime?

Reply: In the meantime, time means. It means more and more.

Question: Listen. Listen to me. That's piss. That's prattle. That's not philosophy; and if it is, it's page one smartass stuff from an Open University primer. So don't pull rank with me. Besides, I happen to know that you came out of college with a catastrophic degree.

Reply: Afterwards, the boy-friend looked at his John Lennon spectacles in the long grass, where a spittle spider hung in a ball of foam on the curve of the left lens. His girl-friend gave him her pantihose because it was a hot day, and they said nothing as they walked back to the apple-peel and the bottle-tops of the picnic party. But that night in his bedroom the boy-friend took her tights from the pocket of his jacket, and held them to his face, and inhaled them. Again and again.

Question: That's a bit strong, isn't it? A bit, you know, for a family book. It's not Dostoevsky or D. H. Lawrence. It's a digest. Now a digest can be this or that, and it often is, but the one thing it can't be is, well, indigestible.

Reply: A digest. Blasts from a Baedeker. Bearings from a Blue Guide.

Question: A Blue Guide, yes; but not a very Blue Guide. Your memories are so highly-strung, so strung out.

Reply: You're right. They are. And that's because the memory holds onto whatever the wind hauls up and hurls at it, the way that a barbed-wire fence at a field clings to a cellophane sandwich wrapper, a scrap of sheep's wool, a morsel of yellow rubber from the wellington boot of a beagler who stumbled as he jumped it. These are trifles, tiny things; but they are the letters of an alphabet by means of which the memory inscribes its silences.

Question: Your editor's going to love this. It's going to crinkle his coffee. I can see him thanking God that Wicklow's a W, right at the back of the book behind Waterford and Wexford, where nobody's likely to look. Tell me this and tell me no more. Have we been talking about the same place at all?

Reply: We have, surely. But a place is always the sum of mostly unuttered – and many unutterable – displacements as well, the semi-literate shadow-side of personal hurt and personal healing. What you realise but don't recognise, because your brain is all mind and no minding, because you think in terms of making a reconnaissance instead of keeping a rendezvous, is that Wicklow is awash with the tears and semen of tens of thousands of Dubliners down through the decades. There's happiness, yes, there's helium in the atmosphere. The hilltop tin-mine tower spears the sky like a primitive phallus, and why not? There's eating and drinking to be had here, from icicles off a drystone wall in January to hashish brownies in an Indian summer. When it snows in the winter, the kids clamber up the slopes below the Hellfire Club in their ravelled balaclavas and their burst sheepskin gloves. The middle-class kids have toboggans bought in Interlaken or the duty-free at Zurich; the working class make do with trays their parents got as wedding presents. Or a car door off a wreck in Lugnaquilla.

Question: It brings me back. It brings me back to the time I used to toboggan. On a toboggan, of course.

Reply: In the first few weeks of May, the month of the Mother of God, the mums and dads from every parish in the diocese bring their wee ones to the woodlands, be it the broad-leaf or the cash-crop conifers, for First Communion photographs. I was there once on an overcast afternoon when it was almost dark because of the low cloud-level, and from behind each and every spruce a small girl stepped out, a child of seven in a bridal dress and veil, her hands in a pose of prayer. A mother in a pillbox hat was waiting for a Polaroid picture to develop. She was staring at the film as if she were studying an area of water where a drowned body was slowly surfacing. But the child never stirred. And I thought of the body and blood of Jesus of Nazareth, the host and the wine that lay in her stomach with toast and ice-cream, like a yellow star stitched to a Brownie's blouse.

Question: You have a bit of religion in you somewhere. I suppose that's something.

Reply: Snowballs and snowmen where the beaux of eighteenth-century Dublin society bet on the Dutch balloonists lifting over the slates of Merrion Square; and mass-produced mother-of-pearl purses for the tiny tots sticking out their tongues at the altar rail. That's the sunny side, the side that faces south. But there's another. Because Wicklow is also an exercise yard for a million captive metropolitans. So it's not just a station platform without tickets or turnstiles; it's a Stations of the Cross for men and women with sensible shoes and photochromic glasses that blacken as the daylight strengthens, for men and women whose inner lives, whose valleys of barley, are hidden from view by guises, disguises, the sand and ice of their outsides. They come here with their mortgages, their coronaries, their desertions. They come to find their bearings, and to bear bravely whatever it is they find. They come because they're breaking up, because they're breaking down, because they've no idea that brokenness is itself a kind of breakthrough. Or at least that it can be. Sometimes. Somehow. God knows how.

Question: God may know, but does he feel?

Reply: Yes. On the other hand, a pathologist informs me that he would have felt less and less after about three hours, and nothing at all by the time he lost consciousness.

Question: I'm not talking about Palestine. I'm talking about the Sugar Loaf and the Sallygap. I'm talking about Glendalough. Now nobody goes to Glendalough because they've got a moral migraine or they're in the District Court on Wednesday. They go because it's only fifteen miles away, and they'd feel a right clot if they met an American tourist who'd flown in from Oklahoma, and they had to admit that they'd never been there. Or they drive down because the baby doesn't cry so much in the car. And there's nothing wrong with that. But you've this way of trying to turn meat and potatoes into bread and wine.

Reply: Glendalough was a centre of work and worship, piety and prayer, throughout the golden age of Celtic Christianity.

Question: Absolutely.

Reply: Its ruins still stand today in a natural setting as lush and lovely as where they shot *The Last Valley*, the movie about the religious wars in seventeenth-century Europe, with Michael Caine and Omar Sharif.

13 Bed and Breakfast, Bray, Co. Wicklow

Question: The witch they burned was a Page Three girl. I recognised her.

Reply: Glendalough was a major university with an international student body from as far afield as Poland and Portugal, at a time when Oxford was only a bit of a brook where a couple of cowherds munched magic mushrooms when they weren't delousing each other.

Question: Now you're talking. Attaboy.

Reply: A woman went there on the summer solstice two years ago. Not one of her friends could quite believe that her black, beautiful hair was natural; but it was. At seventy years of age, she had even thought about using a grey rinse. Would a chemist's have it? Sometime soon she would ask her actor friend how he aged himself for the part of Doctor Chasuble in the Wilde play she could never remember the name of.

Question: *An Ideal Husband.*

Reply: But now it was midsummer, and she walked among the headstones towards the nineteenth-century grave that had her whole née name on it. The poor woman had died at forty-two, if she was subtracting correctly. Childbirth, maybe, or tuberculosis. But not Alzheimer's. Definitely not Alzheimer's.

She bends down to pick up a coin that looks like a twenty-pence piece, but it's foreign, light, perhaps Middle Eastern. Strange that somebody else can make sense out of all those squiggles, as simple as ABC to a child in Constantinople, who may never have heard of Ireland and the terrible things that happen in it.

The hospital held its fire-drill at ten, so it was two hours before they found him wandering in an outsize geriatric diaper among the rose-beds on the corner of the coast road. This was the man whose knowledge of Maimonides had so astonished the Reform rabbi that he told her he would never again assume anything about a gentile; the man whose party piece had been a perfectly accented whirlwind of wisecracks from the Marx brothers, and who stood at the bedroom window each winter morning while the tits took peanuts from the palms of his hands.

She lets the coin drop onto the gravel.

What am I going to do?

Question: I'm lost. I'm confused.

Reply: That's good. Confusion is the first step to blessedness. The second is harder because the road multiplies into a spaghetti junction. Some of the signs say Ism; some of the signs say Ing. Trust them.

Question: Where do they lead?

Reply: Toward a horizon that always recedes as you approach it. Toward the maturity of utter bewilderment. To be sure, there are higher states, but none with a keener knack for keeping body and soul together. For the terrible truth is, if you want to fall in love, you must first of all fall. And I learned that in Wicklow too.

Question: You did not. You learned that sort of blather at Berkeley, where the National Guard had to turn the water-cannon on those gits with beards and bandannas.

Reply: No, I learned it in Wicklow. When I was a child, staying in my godfather's home, a house whose collection of books unhoused me for the rest of my life; a house where I discovered that the rest of your life is a contradiction in terms.

Question: That's the sort of stuff that sells books about Ireland. That's what the punter pays for. I can hear the to-do round the tills in Waterstone's; I can see the Michelin motorist put-puttering in second gear round the Vale of Avoca, arrowing your assortment of helpful hints with a Type 3 pencil. No doubt about it: you've put the place on the map. I shouldn't be surprised if you've put it in the atlas.

Reply: I was there once. In Avoca, I mean. I went down there with two other teachers and a coach-load of schoolboys. One of the teachers sat up front with the driver, to read her Wilbur Smith novel.

Question: Women don't read Wilbur Smith novels. They read novels by men with names like Dominique de la Croix or Gertrude Stormsson; or they read books called *Amino Acids: An Assault on Anxiety* or *PMT – The Scapegoat Sickness*. But they don't read Wilbur Smith.

Reply: This one did. But the whole time she was reading, she never turned the page. She kept looking at the same two pages. And I thought to myself: either this part of the story is explosive, and the same place falls open every time in the newsagent's shop, or else this woman who's got the guts never to pluck her eyebrows is away in another world. I hoped for her sake it was habitable.

Question: You sound like Stacy Keach when you say that. Did you ever think of writing for TV?

Reply: The other teacher was at the back of the bus, chatting to some of the children. If you watched who he talked to, you could tell which of them had domestic difficulties, because he singled out the little lads who'd had to look up long words in the dictionary. Words like infidelity, liquidation, carcinoma of the rectum.

Question: He had his work cut out.

Reply: Each of the boys belonged to primary classes with names instead of numbers, the names of extinct species: elk, woolly mammoth, sabre-toothed tiger. Accordingly, they behaved, thank God, in a prehistoric manner. Because I like kids who can do that. After all, they have seventy years of deodorised mousse ahead of them, and not knowing which knife to start with in a nice restaurant, until it reaches the point where they'd sooner commit homicide than fart audibly at a cocktail party. So I didn't mind when they saluted a bus full of Bavarian matrons with storm-trooper slogans, or when the

16 Country fair, Co. Wicklow

ten-year-old took out his glass eye in front of the waitress. But the place itself pissed me off. I don't quite know why. Perhaps it was because I'd never much cared for the poet himself, for Tom Moore, with whom the whole scenic sweep of the area is associated. But it was more than that. Besides, the poor bastard's been given a hard press, poor-mouthed as a slyboots, a sycophant. The truth is, every Irish writer living in England is a cultural adulterer, eating two dinners and starving to death. And the trek from one country to another, whether from Mayo to Mayfair or from Wicklow to the West End, is such an intricate job of navigation that it makes the *Odyssey* look like the shortest distance between two points.

Anyhow, that was a day for decisions. When we left, we three teachers, each left something behind. One of us left a lover, one of us left a job, one of us left a tip. Twelve months later, a plane touched down in San Francisco, and I got off. I got off minus my baggage, trunks and a suitcase, because they'd been derailed at Heathrow and sent to Scotland. So I stood at a bus stop with a typewriter, two bottles of Tipp-Ex, and a copy of *Mayfair*.

Question: But you found your feet?

Reply: My feet are the only part of me that I can ever claim to have found. They're wherever the ground is.

Question: So what happened?

Reply: There's a café on the corner of Sacramento in downtown San Francisco. Inside, close to the fishtank, there's a fellow in white. He's sipping a *cappuccino*. He's writing a lecture. A lecture about the sense of place in the Irish imagination. Yeats, Synge, Joyce — a busman's holiday. He looks up, looks out. The breeze has freshened. On the wire stacks at the kiosk newspapers flick fast. The fellow in white can read the titles: the *Wall Street Journal*, the *San Francisco Chronicle, Hustler,* the *Wicklow People*.

Question: Get away.

Reply: When he's given his lecture to the sophomore students, the fraternity jocks and the girls in their boob tubes and their espadrilles, he'll go home and cook traditional Irish cuisine — chicken and chips — for his Filipino flatmate. And afterwards, a student will call with a late assignment and he'll pour her a glass of Christian Brother port, and she'll check out the postcards on the wall over his pillow, postcards of lakes and mountains, of shingle beaches and rhododendrons, of skies and sunsets that are one part aquamarine and two parts aerosol paintspray in a studio.

'Is that the place where you grew up?' she asks him.

'No,' he tells her. 'No. It's just a place where I grew.'

18 Early days beside the cigarette factory, Belfast, Co. Antrim

COUNTY ANTRIM

Anne Devlin

The wheat came from Manitoba, it came into the docks and was taken to the flour-mill at Percy Street in St Peter's Parish – Isaac Andrews & Sons. Here the wheat was sucked into the machinery that would turn it into flour. The wheat from Manitoba was the best wheat. I never saw the wheat myself but I did see the flour it became; it covered my father in a fine white dust from head to foot.

According to my father, his family moved in 1850 from the Tyrone side of Lough Neagh round to the Antrim side and entered the city of Belfast via Randalstown. Moving from the country to the city for work: it was not exactly the lyrical journey of simple farming folk or the agricultural worker from the wheatfields to the flour-mills.

'Wheatfields in Tyrone? It's a bit wet!' was all my father would say. Which brings me to the wheat from Manitoba.

Once or twice when he was on night-work, my mother and I would go to the Mill with his supper and wait amidst the hum of machinery and the chorus of pigeons – there were hundreds of them on the roof above the flour-yard – we would wait in the gatekeeper's lodge, a small room with a gas fire, full of dry sacks and a wall of keys. Then my father would arrive grinning in his overalls and cap. That was the nearest I came to nature as a place: the dust of the Manitoba grain on my father's overalls in the gatekeeper's lodge at a flour-mill in Percy Street.

Percy Street ran between the Shankill and Falls Roads, situated at the Falls Road end, and the flour-mill employed both Catholics and Protestants. At a later time in 1969 during another night-shift at the mill Catholic families escaped, helped by men on night-shift, across the rooftops from their burning houses to the safety of the flour-mill. But my father wasn't there, he left his job at Isaac Andrews & Sons in February 1969 when he became the Member of Parliament for Falls. And Percy Street became a battlefield on the nights of 12th, 13th and 14th August between Catholic and Protestant crowds. Milk-crates of Molotov cocktails were stacked up by the flour-mill gates. Now that I've got that out of the way I can go on – this is not what I wanted to write about, it never has been. But I am no poet of loughs and glens or lakes and fern, though I wish in my heart that I were. I had an urban childhood and no 'blooming' landscape that I could celebrate – except in the most pejorative sense (until perhaps . . . nor did I ever . . .) – for Belfast, County Antrim was a place of political intelligence of which I was precocious, and a place of industry of which I had no part.

Until perhaps . . . somewhere in the attic in this house is a map of Dunluce and Dunsevrick, and a townland marked at the bend of the River Bann, east bank, between Coleraine, three miles out, and Ballymoney, five miles; the field next to the Mountsandel Fort, not visible but marked on the map drawn up by a British serving officer in 1830. Given to me as a wedding present. My relationship with North Antrim began at that house, a low-lying bungalow overlooking the River Bann and obscured from the Kilrea Road by Loughan Island. When I first became aware of the country dark, and elderflowers, and wild daffodils and pike. And every morning I'd drive off along the

Ballybogey Road to work. The sound of magpies – the mating cry; I watched wild rabbits boxing and saw a badger's lair; went nude bathing at Castlerock and took a much-sought kiss on White Park Bay. Then I found a landscape I could celebrate, but, it seems, only after I was torn away from it.

Nor did I ever . . . feel that it would last? Was that it? Nor did I ever live in Antrim or the countryside again. I have returned to the urban landscape of my childhood – only in a different city.

I cannot now live in Antrim, so much was discovered and then lost there. Land-locked in England I still remember those great beaches: Portstewart Strand, White Park Bay, Downhill and Castlerock; some of the best beaches in the world and some of the worst weather. After the divorce, a new lover and motherhood have healed me. I go back on a visit. I am sitting with Medbh and her children on Ballycastle beach.

There were other sounds – dogs barking on the river bank – the sounds of a nightmare. Medbh is telling me about a house she is going to buy in North Antrim. I am hearing the other sounds above the sounds of the gulls. A slow tread of a Land Rover watching the bungalow for our own protection. The only Catholics for miles – I should say Catholic: a mixed marriage. And that motorbike – has it just slowed down?

'What's wrong?' Medbh asks.

'It sounds a bit isolated to me. I like to see the lights of the house next door.'

On the other hand I could live on a sea-shore anywhere.

My son, an oedipal four, angry because I am not talking to him, has wandered off along the beach, naked as a shrimp, so far away now that I am worried and tear off after him. Medbh's words are drowned momentarily, in the Atlantic's tumultuous roar.

Antrim does not exist in a place for me any more than nature or industry exists in a place: it exists as a history. A history of moments that we occupied, or were driven out of, or returned to.

During the Belfast hunger strikes of May 1981, I was staying in Devon with friends at a house on a beach near Padstow. I had a recurring dream that I was running along a familiar entry in Belfast, in some danger, when I came to the back door of our house on the Grosvenor Road. The dream was a recurring one of failure: I had often run in those entries as a child, and in my dreams after we left that house and moved to Andersonstown when I was thirteen I frequently tried to run back to my grandmother's house and never succeeded. This time, however, after all those years – joy, the door was open. I ran into the yard and found the house was full of light and all the doors were open. I had found the house again – the core of my childhood self, safe, and waiting with all the lights on. I found my old room and old bed, and as I lay down to sleep I was suddenly aware of another presence in the room. I knew when I turned around to look my grandmother would be beside me. So I turned around, and the action of turning woke me up. And I found myself staring around the room in the beach house at Padstow. I had no sense of loss, but of the good mother watching over me. A few hours later I received a phone call from my father explaining that my entire

21 Street party, Lepper Street, Belfast, Co. Antrim

22 Tiger's Bay, Belfast, Co. Antrim

family had moved out of their house in Andersonstown, away from the anger of their neighbours.

My father did not support the politics of the hunger strikes.

Bruno Bettelheim says when he was in the concentration camps (Dachau and Buchenwald) he frequently dreamed of picnics with his family. When he escaped to Chicago in 1945, he fell asleep and dreamed of concentration camps. Our dreams may be a way of strengthening our psyche for troubles ahead; but Bettelheim did actually escape. All those picnics were already there for him. What he did not leave behind was the terrifying and despairing landscape of the terror itself.

I cannot help that my imagination dreamed a repossession when my parents lost their house. I cannot help that my imagination took this loss for a gain – a return to the country of the self. I only know that the self is not the same as autobiography: I am the sum of all the lives and events that have touched my own.

Once I wandered along White Park Bay with a man who changed my life, from whom I later became estranged. In another part of County Antrim in a place totally bound up with memories of childhood health, two groups of rioters confronted each other in front of the flour-mill gates, and that also changed my life.

It is not Antrim, but the self that is the country. And the self is inexhaustible. That is not to say that there isn't a landscape, a place in Ireland, that I could celebrate: a moment I was never driven out of. One day in May, walking along a road towards a headland, I looked back and saw my new lover walking towards me, head thrown back in the wind, beneath the sky and the trees, our son was five months old and the shore was ahead of us. Everything about that moment is timeless.

The same place, in sight of the Mournes, where my sister took off her city shoes and walked in the sand, twenty-four hours before the birth of her first child; before she went to Australia. At night the Liverpool boat passes so close to this coast, the red and green lights of port and starboard are clearly visible. And the waves carry the hum of the engines to the very edge of the house door. You can stand in front of the cottage and feel the ground throb and the sea swell. In daylight too, a captain on one of those ferries always sounds the ship's horn when he returns because his mother lives in these parts – to say 'I'm safely home.' This is the place I could live. I call it back – I am there now standing on the road watching with the mountains and the sky, the man walking towards me, listening to the sea, the ebb and flow of its constancy to this particular shore: the constant self. I lay myself the full length of the shore for him – somewhere in County Down.

24 On the flag, Belfast, Co. Antrim

25 Christmas Eve, selling lighters, Belfast, Co. Antrim

26 Bridesmaid, Belfast, Co. Antrim

27 Travelling children, Glen Road, Belfast, Co. Antrim

COUNTY KILKENNY

Thomas Kilroy

Like a nail on a map, the Normans made their mark on Kilkenny. Not once but twice. Firstly on their startling arrival in the twelfth century, single knights encased in chain-mail with their flocks of Welsh archers, technology invading pastoral. They drove the native chieftains northwards towards the foothills of Slieve Bloom and planted the countryside with their castles and keeps. They re-entered the place in very different fashion nearly five hundred years later when they were dispossessed by Cromwell. Driven out of their homes as rebels, the descendants of those first conquerors sank back into the mere Irish, assimilated into the race like so many other invaders of Ireland. Grace, Tobin, Walsh, Purcell, Freaney, Prendergast, Comerford and the most famous Irish Norman name of all, Butler, the one family which remained loyal to England throughout and thereby kept its title, Ormonde, into our own times. The list sounds like part of a Kilkenny hurling team, as indeed it should. There are also those other Norman surnames which have suffered a different kind of assimilation, like Ragget and Viper, that are now preserved only in place-names.

The Normans gave the place its stony base, as it were. Perhaps they also contributed the characteristically long, bony Kilkenny face, perhaps even that flat, utilitarian accent. Certainly there is Norman blood in the makings of those efficient, solid farmers and merchants of the county today. One of the colours of this county is black. Black marble, black limestone when polished by scuffing, the Black Abbey, the Black River; while to the north there are the black coalfields of Castlecomer.

But the other colour of Kilkenny is amber, a brilliantly exotic contrast which is nowhere more marked than in the thin vertical lines of black and amber of the Kilkenny hurling jersey. I like to think that those colours, in their contrast, encapsulate not only the character of the place but something of the peculiar blend of style in Kilkenny hurling itself. It has its airy grace, the flick, tap, swing of the stick, the effortless accuracy from sideline or midfield with or without the use of hand-ball. This is what the crowds delight in at Croke Park on All-Ireland Hurling Final Sunday. And the player, as often as not, is a figure of apparent frailty, as great Kilkenny forwards so often are. But behind all this is a thin, implacable obduracy, the black line, as if lyricism had been matched to penury.

When I was a boy, with socks down over my boots, hurling backs and forwards on the fair green in Callan, there used to be a taunt: 'Sure, he's only a hair-oil hurler!' This was sometimes directed at the literal specimen itself, hair plastered in Brylcreem in anticipation of a night out at Bill Egan's cinema. But more often it was directed at some fancy artiste who wafted about on the edge of the slaughter going on in the square, prancing like a ballerina and picking off points while the rest of us ground deeper into the muck. Both the style and the taunt are typical of Kilkenny, Antaeus trying to pull down Icarus.

Look at the map. The county is shaped by three of the most limpid rivers of Ireland: the Suir to the west in Tipperary, the Barrow to the east in Carlow, while down

30 Family after Mass, Co. Kilkenny

through the centre of the county flows Kilkenny's own river, the Nore. All three meet in confluence at the butt end of the county. The Nore joins the Barrow near New Ross and, later, the two sisters join the Suir at Waterford, the estuary which cuts off Kilkenny from the sea. But although it is land-locked Kilkenny takes its water spirit from these rivers. These are rich pasture rivers and before pollution they gave the sense of being swollen with the bounty of the land through which they flowed. In this southern corner of the county where these rivers meet is an enchanting landscape of river, hill and meadow bottoms, especially between Inistioge and the sea. It also happens to be great hurling territory but that may be accidental.

To find the delicacy and lightness within or behind the solid shapes and heavy verdure of Kilkenny is to discover the essence of the place. In recent years this has become the goal of an international colony of artists and craft-workers who have made their homes and studios here: potters, weavers, smiths, sculptors, painters. That a movement like this should grow here, one dedicated to marrying art and pragmatic skills, is entirely apt. In the local character pragmatism is never far behind any gesture, however inconsequential or carefree. Kilkenny people like results.

Two contemporary artists in particular have worked across the face of this county, although the Kilkenny paintings represent but a fraction of their substantial output. Tony O'Malley is a native of Callan. He has returned again and again from his other home in St Ives to paint in this locality. He has a massive series of paintings inspired by the virtually anonymous master stone-carvers of Jerpoint Abbey. The canvas is made to bear the texture and definition of the stone, its chiselled, stained and weathered surface. These are not just memorials, although the reverence for the dead carvers is manifest. Nor are they just distillations of another art-form in paint, yet the bond across time between the living artist and his avatars is unmistakable. It is based upon a shared lucidity. Barrie Cooke, on the other hand, has simply lived for a while in Kilkenny. Among his Kilkenny works is a sequence of very beautiful paintings of the River Nore. They are paintings of greenness, of the great load of the river quantified by the density of a single colour. These are obviously very different artists but each in his own way has caught something intrinsic to this place, its gravity and the elegance which lightens it.

32 The interloper, Kilkenny town, Co. Kilkenny

COUNTY LIMERICK

Michael Hartnett

No large rivers flow south in County Limerick; they flow north towards their sacred mother, the Shannon. And there are only two of any consequence – the Deel and the Maigue, which bring with them almost all the heritage and the history of the county. The county itself, like many Irish counties, is an Ireland in miniature – hills, bogs, a plain, some woods; and a diversity of people. County Limerick is not a single entity: Limerick city and, say, West Limerick, are virtually mutually exclusive of each other when it comes to custom, attitude and even accent.

The city, originally a Viking settlement, is slowly rising out of the seedy shambles of its past – you may, in a walk of five minutes, move from a rubbish-strewn housing estate with the occasional untethered horse or goat wandering about, into a beautiful Georgian square. Indeed the city is as diverse as the county itself. I love almost all of the city. It has some excellent pubs and restaurants – but there is one item, which when I see it in a butcher's shop window makes me want to flee. It is the local delicacy, packet and tripe. Packet is a blood-pudding and looks like the partially decomposed member of a jackass and indeed, when cooked with the glutinous grey tripe, probably tastes like one. And so to the open air.

Flowing west, the River Shannon begins to widen beneath the walls of King John's castle, and leaving the city behind seems to reach out to embrace the Limerick and Clare shores, until it becomes again what it was up-country, magnificent water. It soon receives on its southern bank the Maigue and the Deel – once great rivers for brown trout but alas, because of the greed and carelessness of a few inland farmers and industries, 'not the rivers they used to be'. The Shannon ignores the ugly chimneys of the Mungret cement factory and soon comes to one of County Limerick's most magical and, in the evening, most mysterious ruins: Dromore Castle. It looks like the Rock of Cashel transposed and was built in the last century. It was soon abandoned because of the cost of upkeep but lately 'rediscovered' and used as the location for Neil Jordan's film *High Spirits* – appropriately, a ghost story.

Soon the river laps Foynes (once a busy port and landing-place for the early seaplanes), the name of which in Gaelic is An Fhaing, said to derive from the Latin *vagina*, because of the shape of the inlet. And so, on to one of my favourite towns, Glin, the home of the Fitzgeralds, the Knights of Glin, who have remained in possession of the lands and castle since Norman times.

But this prosaic account gives little notion of the beauty that the Shannon skirts on her way to the Atlantic.

South of Glin is the village of Athea (my grandfather was born there in about 1850). The roads become narrow and one enters the 'hidden Ireland' of West Limerick. This

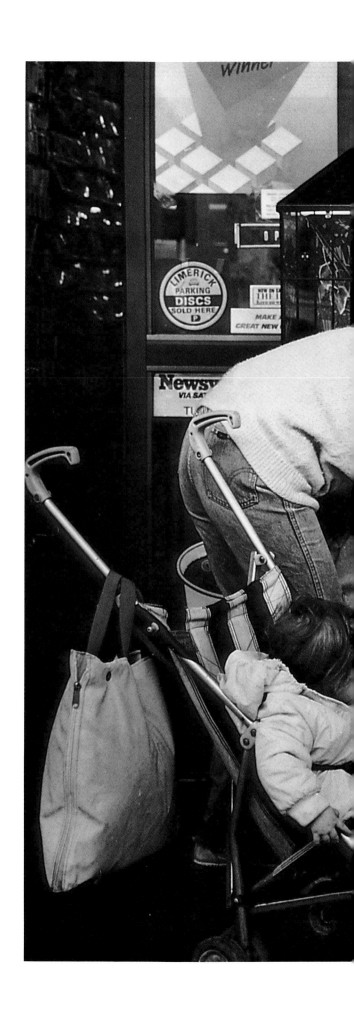

34 Father, mother and children, Co. Limerick

is boggy and hilly country where ravens dance overhead, and owls, marsh-harriers and even falcons fly unmolested. No tourists come here, fortunately, though they miss the best of real Irish music played here in pubs and community centres in Ardagh, Abbeyfeale, Ashford, Tournafulla and Broadford. For this is the western edge of Sliabh Luachra (the Rushy Mountain), with its own personal style of speech and fiddle-playing. This was and is the home of poets and ballad-makers also. Almost every parish has its poet, celebrating local beauties (both topographical and human) in what some moderns might consider unsophisticated verse; but if these ballads are examined, it can be seen that the metres, the use of half-rhyme and internal rhyme are far from 'unsophisticated'. More than once I have been challenged to a 'rhymin' competition' – which means that two poets publicly (usually in a public house!) must out-rhyme each other, the loser buying the pints. Needless to say, the 'verses' born out of such ventures make little sense – the rhyme is all. The last such challenge I received was in Jack Macks' pub in Abbeyfeale in the mid 1970s. I hope the custom is not dead (even though I think I lost!).

Abbeyfeale, one of the best drinking towns in Ireland, is the point from where we turn eastwards towards Killmallock and another 'hidden Ireland'.

East Limerick is again 'another county'. Even the surnames of the people indicate their origins here and nowhere else. A Ryan is certain to be from this area, as is a Kiely, say. And village-names like Bruff, Doon, Caherconlish and Pallas sound almost exotic to the people of the west.

Here also lies the only lake in the county, Lough Gur, near Herbertstown. It is a small, horseshoe-shaped piece of water, surrounded by low, protective hills of limestone. It is one of the most beautiful parts of County Limerick. The lake area contains the remains of the dwelling-places of early man – huts, ramparts and crannogs, those fortified artificial islands built in the lake and connected to the shore apparently by causeways which lay beneath the surface to deceive any would-be attackers. Types of the older dwellings have recently been reconstructed *in situ*. Go there in the evening when the visitors have gone and watch the swans.

It is said that in this area *poitín* (poteen), that crystal-clear, magic prototype of its sickly cousin whiskey, is distilled. Fables, myths, rumours abound in Ireland – so don't believe all you hear or read about the origin of any particular bottle of *poitín*. I was once given a quart of same, said to have been distilled in the Doon area. It had been aged and was equal in taste and bouquet to any Highland malt. Alas, I over-indulged (a dangerous thing to do) and discovered that there *are* pookas, banshees and leprechauns in Ireland!

If we ramble back again to Abbeyfeale via Killmallock – capital of Ireland briefly in the seventeenth century – and turn north-east towards Barna Gap, we can see, almost a thousand feet below, the central plain of the county – and indeed the richest part, being as it is a section of the Golden Vale. The Normans fell in love with it, fought for it and won it and nailed it down with their many castles. They left their names and descendants here (all Fitzs, Brownes, Walshes, etc.). Palatine Germans were settled here in the eighteenth century and there is still a thriving Protestant population round

38 Carrots, Co. Limerick

and about Rathkeale and Adare – which last village is a pice of Devonshire incongruously set among rambling, unplanned Irish settlements. This an area of big, walled estates and pink-coated huntsmen on their fine locally-bred hunters, watched with some resentment and much admiration by the people of Newcastle West with its lovely river and demesne and its innumerable grumbling pubs.

But that's Limerick, city and county – a microcosm of the contradiction that is Ireland.

40 Young lovers, Co. Meath

COUNTY MEATH

Francis Stuart

My parents came from County Antrim but my father died soon after I was born, my mother was estranged from the family and left the North while I, an orphan, was adopted by an aunt in Meath. At a whitewashed farmhouse on the banks of a small river at its heart I spent much of my childhood. Tenderly it embraced me on walks and drives in a pony trap down leafy tracks, some of whose obscure names remain in my memory after all the years, such as Sheridan's Lane, while I often cannot recall familiar ones from the other day. The river Nanny, half-hidden by hazels and willows, wound its way the few miles to what seemed the faraway sea. And the hill of Bellewstown, Croca Fotha in Irish, legendary and ancient beyond other more imposing hills, broke from the flat horizon and brooded over the countryside. And, giving it for me an added importance, the postman trudged down through fields of grazing cattle with letters for my mother and aunt that were laid beside their places on the breakfast table.

Of the greater glories of the county I came to learn much later: the Boyne, most fabled of Irish rivers, the Passage graves at Fournock, archaeologically famous in Western Europe, dating, like those at Newgrange, around 1,800 BC, the Hill of Tara where the semi-mythical king of the De Dannans is said to have reigned at about the same time, and where later appeared the Milesians from Iberia.

It was not, however, the wonders of its past that drew me back there with my late wife, Madeleine, after twenty years' exile from Ireland. My childhood memories impelled me to buy a cottage with our last few pounds with a view of the same hill, though from another aspect, which had often figured in my thoughts of 'home'.

It was in the ten or twelve years we spent there, just overlapping the 1960s, that I got to know Meath — at least the part of it within cycling range, though in the latter years we had a car — intimately.

It is not a 'scenic' part of the island and its narrow side-roads between high hedges, as they were then, were frequented morning and evening by dairy herds on their way to the byre for milking, rather than by tourists.

In our first years the limits of our expeditions were the county capital, Navan, to the north, Kilmessan in summer to bathe by the old Bective mill, Laytown for the horse-races on the strand once a year and the village of Dunshaughlin to take a bus to Dublin.

It was in and around the cottage whose address — that of the townland — was the Reask, that we assimilated the aura of Meath most intensely. How often, anxious with money or less defined worries, I went to stand at the low stone wall that separated our half-acre from the surrounding land to gaze across the huge pasture, subconsciously seeking to prove the truth of Patrick Kavanagh's lines about 'the fields that heal the humble'.

At night we listened to the heavy breathing of the bullocks as they rubbed against the back window-sill of our bedroom. And before we received a grant to install piped

42 Early morning, Laytown, Co. Meath

water, it was also healing to go to the well which we had discovered beneath a tangle of brambles, to stare in surprise into what seemed a dry cavity, so still and limpid was the water as to be invisible, before lowering a bucket.

As a novelist, I had to work and make what then was a meagre living. Where I have done my writing, mostly rooms in a city, has not mattered very much, but the fictions I composed at the Reask – a novel, *Blacklist Section H*, in which Meath is not so much as mentioned, and another, *Memorial*, part of which is set in the cottage and its gardens, where an old man muses as he passes the gravestones of household pets – grew out of those sheltered, fertile pastures.

There were glimpses of foxes trotting from covert to covert and, disturbingly, of horses and hounds on the days when the Ward Union hunt met in the neighbourhood. On two successive Easter mornings a hare appeared on the strip of lawn between cottage and vegetable garden, and one tragic evening we found a nest of leverets in a hedge that our tabby had ravaged and from which we saved one of the tiny creatures.

We were socially isolated. Meath farmers and labourers have none of the open-heartedness or even interest in strangers that do, say, the people of Clare. We were hermits in our Meath refuge, with few visitors and far from the literary life of Dublin.

In one sense, perhaps a superficial one, those were years in which nothing much happened, and yet some of what 'happened' lingers more vividly in mind and heart than do the historic events I experienced during the Second World War.

It would be very painful to return to the Reask. Even driving through Meath on a main road brings back a flood of nostalgia. There are precious graves there, one of a pet that was the closest to us of them all, and that of my mother who died there and who is buried in a small cemetery in a field at Curragha. Because of the fertility of the soil the grave, and the small stones with which we surrounded it pending getting together the sum for a tombstone, became obliterated and we never managed to find it again.

That is the indifference of nature, but the nature of County Meath has its own tenderness. Here is a passage from the novel I mentioned, *Memorial*:

> The cultivation of the garden had for long been one of the ways I hoped to keep myself 'sane'. Between digging and weeding I took a rest at one of the two limestone slabs. At times I could immerse myself in the silence where those whom the stones commemorated were gone. They were present in a secluded corner of a remembering mind and, in most cases, nowhere else in the world. There was John Lodwick, less utterly traceless because he had been a writer, though a comparatively obscure one, dying young, and one of his novels might still be somewhere taken from a shelf. I too became patient and undemanding in their company as they inhabited that plot in Meath, to which I imaginatively transported my dead friend.

The garden got dug and weeded, groundsel, dandelion – larger than any I have seen elsewhere and devoured by our rabbits – bright green tufts of 'Scotch grass' were uprooted while I passed from the company of the dead with regained quietude.

46 Work and play, Laytown, Co. Meath. Previous page: The Laytown Races

47 After the race, Laytown, Co. Meath

48 Co. Donegal

COUNTY DONEGAL

Brian Moore

I drive through the village of Creeslough with the reckless confidence of a blind man in remembered territory. I take the left fork at the edge of the village down a small road which leads to Duntally, my uncle's farm. Unlike my native Belfast, Creeslough has not changed and now, after fifty years of exile and wanderings, I am back in that enchanted place of my early summers.

Of course, my uncle is long dead. When I reach the turn of the road and look up at the house, it is not the same house. There are no chickens in the yard, no pigs rooting behind the byre, no cows, no donkey. I get out of the car, suddenly ill at ease. Am I mistaken? Was Duntally further down the road? Is this the small, circumscribed yet illimitable world in which I spent my summers from the ages of nine to thirteen?

And then, in the quiet of an autumn morning, I hear the waterfall. I run across the road, climb up on the ditch and push aside the rain-wet hazel-nut bushes. There it is below me, the froth of white water tumbling over greenish rocks to fall into a hidden pool of water far below. And, always, that mysterious watery roar, night and day, day and night, year in, year out. Times have changed, Ireland has changed. I am old. But the waterfall is there. And since it is there I know that up this road I will find the ruined castle.

I drive up the road in my rented car. When I was last here one rarely saw a car. I walked everywhere or sometimes got a ride on the crossbar of a neighbour's bicycle. That long journey from the farm to the castle is now over in minutes as the car passes a new sign telling me that Doe Castle was built in 1424 by the warrior MacSwineys and has sheltered such heroes as Red Hugh O'Donnell and Owen Roe O'Neill who sailed back here from Dunkirk in 1642 in a ship containing one hundred Irish veterans of the Spanish wars. Gentrified, with a car-park, its battlements meticulously restored, the castle is now an historical landmark patrolled by camera-bearing German and English tourists.

When I was a boy, Doe castle had no history. It was abandoned, a shelter for cows, its ruined ramparts and winding stone stairs a magical fort in which I could play for hours, alone, hullooing to imaginary allies as I ventured out on its dizzying battlements, pouring imaginary boiling oil on imaginary foes from the secret trapdoor above the drawbridge. And even now as I re-enter its walls, the memory of those shouts, of my feet racing up the winding steps, of the rain lashing across the lough which opens to the sea, of the cows huddled beneath the fireplace of the great hall, floods back into my mind and I know that I am home, in this place which was not my true home, Donegal, my Tir-na-Nog, my land of eternal youth.

The castle, the village, the farm: within that very Irish trinity was the whole world of those childhood summers. I was a city child, a doctor's son, who had known nothing of country life. Donegal was my mother's county. Normally, we spent our summers in rented houses at seaside resorts like Bangor and Portstewart. But now I was out of

Ulster with its sectarian hatreds and discriminations. I was in the Free State, but still, anomalously, in the North. The people here spoke not with the Southern brogues but in the accents familiar to me from the counties of Antrim and Down.

And yet I was in a world where Irish was commonly spoken, that language my mother knew, that language I had never known. I seemed to be in an older Ireland, a place where life was elemental and harsh, yet close to a reality which was timeless and true. I would see a pig slaughtered, its blood running in rivulets in the yard outside the kitchen door. I would see a stallion mount a mare, its hooves scraping at the barrel of her rib-cage, I would see a cow giving birth in the byre, chickens killed with a brutal twist of the neck. I would be butted by yellow-eyed goats, kicked by donkeys when I tried to climb on their backs. I would see people drink tea, not from teacups as in Belfast, but from large china bowls in the eighteenth-century manner. I would sit by the hob of the kitchen turf-fire watching as floury potatoes were doled out from an iron pot to the men coming in from the fields for their noonday dinner. I would watch mice run out in droves from the last unscythed triangle of a field, as the men advanced in a line, cutting corn. I would see long white clay pipes and plugs of tobacco laid out near jugs of poteen at my aunt's wake. And each summer when school term came around I would leave in tears, waving goodbye to Donegal from the back seat of the Letterkenny bus.

Now, an exile who has lived far longer out of Ireland than in it, those scenes remain in my mind, imperfectly yet keenly remembered in a far different way from my confused recollections of Belfast where I was born and bred. It would be many years later, as an adult and an expatriate, that I would explore the roads which led from Creeslough to places I knew only as names in my childhood summers – Dunfanaghy, Carrigart, Bloody Foreland, Killybegs and Donegal town.

In the main square of Donegal town I watch men selling cows on a fair-day and am at once carried back to a lost memory of a day when I stood holding a rope attached to a calf in the main street of Creeslough, waiting for my uncle to come out of the pub where he was celebrating the calf's purchase. Driving along the narrow roads past the rock-strewn, barren fields of the Rosses, I pass ruined, abandoned cottages and remember the emigrant songs people sang around the fire on those long-ago summer evenings. For those were the days when to leave Donegal and sail to America was a wake, a final parting with all one had ever known: family, friends and, above all, this wild, bare, brutal, enchanted landscape.

Unlike those who left then, I come back to stand here, a revenant, seeing the present but remembering a far more vivid past. Can the reality of today change my vision of those long-ago summers? No. Donegal, like the waterfall below Duntally, is Ireland, eternal as the thunder of white water falling endlessly into a hidden pool far below.

51 Beach, Horn Head, Co. Donegal

52 Passing Muckish Mountain, before Dunlewy Lake, Co. Donegal

53 Bogland, Co. Donegal

54 Dunlewy and the Derryveagh Mountains, Co. Donegal

55 From Errigal Mountain, Co. Donegal

56 Lake Nacung, 6.00 a.m., Co. Donegal

58 The family estate, Co. Monaghan

COUNTY MONAGHAN

Eugene McCabe

A hard, bright day; mid winter. Am aware like thirty-one others I should be inside writing, in my case about Monaghan now, and echoes from the vanquished kingdom of Oriel: 'MacMahon country'. Happy enough meantime to be up the north side of the haggard field thinning out an ash-ditch for firewood. Far below, across the river and perched above a disused quarry, a British Army observation post stares down from South Fermanagh, by day a concrete grin, by night its orangey flares sometimes light up the river and surrounding townlands, dead flare-shells parachuting south into ditches, gaps and bottomlands. There now almost ten years. Legionnaires from Britain; a sewagey smell when you check through.

I hear first the yallering, yowling and yahooing of huntsmen, then see them in the church field, running in pincer movement to surround the old graveyard, capped and coated and squelching in wellies after their baying harriers. An Irish Army patrol stops to let them cross the unapproved road. As they emerge I see again the three Fermanagh farms where the sons of Cain (Adam's patriots) committed murder most foul. The hounds reappear in a river bottom between two spiked bridges, throaty hunting cries mixed with yelps, a sound primitive as snipebleat, heronscry or the chill croak of scaldcrow.

For the first time I see the hare near the Priest's Bridge; then a blur as it goes loping towards the lake bottoms of Tirnachinch. Somewhere in those wet acres in 1643 Eoghan Rua O'Neill suffered his first military defeat – end of the Gaelic world: a haunted landscape. The hare goes out of sight followed by hounds and huntsmen. Five minutes later near Benson's round tower I see the hunt again, their cries drowned suddenly by the heavy vibrations of a helicopter, a troop-carrier from Roslea chopping its way across Shannock, home of Thomas Lipton, towards the observation post. I pray: victory for the hare, defeat for the horseless gentry, and decide to go in and make a start.

With what? The obvious? Border country? Drumlin country? 'MacMahon country' is how it is described in seventeenth-century English State Papers. Descendants of Mathghamhain, 'the bear-like person', slain in 1022. And bear-like they had to be, with O'Neill exacting tribute from the north, the Anglo-Normans of the Pale pushing up from the south, caught in a kind of limbo from earliest times. The Valley of the Black Pig, a prehistoric fortified earthen trench, can still be followed by helicopter from Carlingford to the Atlantic. Then as now it sealed off the Kingdom of Ulster. Sometime during childhood my mother (a MacMahon) read us a piece from the *Anglo-Celt*, portions of which she knew by heart thereafter. It described the defeat and expulsion of the Monaghan MacMahons to the barren uplands of Fermanagh, her father's birthplace. 'And that is why to this day in many a poor Fermanagh cabin, when you find the name MacMahon, you invariably find an inborn grace, a natural courtesy of manner rarely encountered elsewhere in this island.' I wholly believed this as a child, half believed it as a man, until the night Philip Moore read a paper about the MacMahons to the Clogher Historical Society.

I brought my mother. For an hour we listened to a tale of intrigue and betrayal, of cattle-raiding and brutality, of greed, murder, burnings and drownings, machiavellian cowboys markedly indifferent to poets and poetry, to Church and religion, no hint anywhere of 'inborn grace and natural courtesy of manner'! On the way home my mother was quiet. Finally she said, 'I'm not certain, dear, that Mr Moore had all his facts right.' History, I agreed, could be dodgy. If you're not there how can you tell, and being there you might tell it differently from the next fellow. She commended my wisdom. In herself gracious and gentle, foolish and subtle, she is long at peace. May she continue thus until we meet in the everlasting, and learn from an infallible source the good or bad news about the MacMahons.

Muineachan, country of the little hills, bundle upon bundle of odd-shaped fields, mounds, forts and keeps, topped by circles of ash and thorn, glacier-carved humps and hollows, creating hundreds of natural amphitheatres and hidden townlands, the whole furnished with lakes and rivers, boglands and bottomlands, hedges of magical blackthorn, deep-dug ditches and some wonderful stands of planter hardwood, all of it accessible by more roads, lanes, tracks, by-roads, canal walks, farm passes, overgrown coachways and obsolete railway sidings than any other area in Western Europe, or so we claim. Lest this seem braggartly, it must be said that the mile of no man's land border road to Drumard (our farm) must be one of the most badger-riddled and bockedy in Western Europe!

The last three decades have brought steel-roofed barns, cemented yards, concrete block farm buildings, silo and slurry pits, gleaming chicken and turkey broiler houses and the long black plastic tunnels of a booming mushroom business, and a more expansionist outlook than Cavan, Sligo, Leitrim, Longford and Donegal put together (according to 1983 EEC figures) and a consequent spin-off in bungalows which seem less unnatural here in the green drumlins than in the stark beauty of Connemara.

The Tudor map of the county looks a bit like Australia kicked sideways. It was drawn up by Henry VIII's natural son, Sir John Perrot, in 1585. Tudor language is still common, with quirks of speech and pronunciation rarely heard elsewhere. 'I'll tell you the kind of fellow he is, you wouldn't know what kind he was!' The border mind, thinking two ways, looking ten ways, conspiratorial, contradictory and cautious. Sir John's map subdivided the county into five baronies: three hundred years later the Great Northern Railway bisected it from Clones to Inniskeen, Kavanagh's country. Some maintain there is a marked difference between people north and south of this line, and cite as example the difference between Clones, and Carrickmacross lace. Clones lace is sturdy and chunky – you can wear it, wash it, boil it and it remains beautiful. Carrickmacross lace delights in fine detail – organdy appliquéd on tulle, purpose-made for billowing in summer windows … northern practicality as against southern lyricism (a strained comparison maybe in a county some twenty miles by forty).

Certainly there was no north/south county thing when the baronies were mapped and named and no change since: Truagh, Dartry, Cremorne, Monaghan and Farney in the south, confiscated and granted by the first Elizabeth – all sixty-seven thousand acres of it! – to her dubious boyfriend the Earl of Essex. Shirley, a direct descendant of the unlucky earl, published his *History of Monaghan* in 1883, a fascinating overlord's view. In it he lists in English and Irish all 1,853 townlands, for example:

Fastry	A wilderness
Anagose	A field of caves
Clonshanco	Meadow of foxes
Tiromeadan	Land of the fool
Lisanore	The fort of tears
Tamlat	A burial place

Shirley's land-agent W. Stuart French arrived from England to this barony at the end of March 1843. His account in *Realities of Irish Life* of that first week is hard to forget. Early in April a crowd of about ten thousand gathered in the main street of Carrickmacross outside the agent's house (now the Louis Convent, begetters and promoters of Carrickmacross lace) demanding a reduction of rent. Shirley sent out Trench, who stood on a chair and told them there could be no reduction:

There was a dead silence when I stopped speaking.

'Down on your knees, boys,' shouted a voice. 'We will ask him once more on our knees!'

And to my horror and amazement the vast crowd, or at least all those in my immediate vicinity, dropped suddenly on their knees, and another dead silence ensued.

There then follows a vivid and frightening description telling how he was beaten, punched and stripped naked until finally, certain that he was near death, he spoke to and won over his attackers. They then chaired and cheered him 'towards Shirley's Castle, the Demesne of Lough Lea'.

Why has this detail from a remote county history haunted not only memory but dreams? Was I abject amongst the kneeling rackrented dispossessed thousands? Did I jostle and claw at Trench? Or was I one of the crowd who admired his courage and saved him from what seemed like certain death? Both? Could I be near-assassin and white knight within the space of an hour? Impossible not to look back and wonder.

Monaghan long ago: Ulster now: heartbreaking analogies. Imperative to look forward to the peace that must someday come. 'Onwards' . . . It was one of Tyrone Guthrie's favourite catch-phrases, the other being 'rise above'. Like Swift a stern critic and great encourager of Ireland and its people, he left his house and estate as a retreat for artists. It flourishes, supported, as he intended, by the Arts Councils of North and South. Among Monaghan notables he ranks as the most gifted and generous the county has ever known. And what of the others? How do you begin to choose between a bishop on the run in penal days, the present managing director of Guinness, an ICA President, a Businesswoman of the Year, James Connolly and Nobby Clarke, street singer and fair-green hawker? Is an eighteenth-century reforming agriculturalist, Samuel ('Premium') Madden, more or less deserving of mention than the long list of the gifted Leslie clan? Are any of them as fascinating as the mad doctor, outcast of another family, who sold placebos round the fairs – farting loudly and shouting slogans like 'Balls is ornaments!'? The resident psychiatrist at St Davnet's has accomplished so much for the health of the county, but being a 'blow-in' he can't be mentioned, nor for that matter the manager of Monaghan Co-op and its vital earning link with every other farming family in the county. Is Sir Charles Gavan Duffy, founder of *The Nation* newspaper and a Knight of Pacific Nationalism, held in more or less esteem by his fellow countymen than our young men who have killed brutally and been brutally killed? The answer we all suspect; few of us would care to see it written down. And then there is Cecil Parke, born in Clones in 1881, the greatest ever Irish sporting all-rounder and now as dead to public memory as Barry McGuigan, World Champion boxer, is alive. Is the fascist General Eoin O'Duffy, a crusading blueshirt in Franco's Spain, more or less heroic than Pat Fee, who took his mother out of the poor-house and wheeled her through Monaghan crusading for bread, pence and shelter till she died in Smithborough in the winter of 1851?

And finally there is the great assemblage of professing religious from the largely unChristlike denominations, and, even bigger, the listed trades and professions, and, still in the majority by thousands, the small farmers of Monaghan – now well off their knees and walking steadily. And their women? The childbearing home-makers, the lace-making shroud-makers who survived the Famine to watch and grieve over their children who have left since in their thousands and still leave, seldom to return. Kavanagh has celebrated the comedy and tragedy of their lives in prose and verse. If the choice of notables created a minor problem, then, for me, he solves it. As a teenager I once followed him up Grafton St wanting desperately to stop him and say something. My nerve failed: I could think of nothing apt. Now forty years later I can write it. He *is* Monaghan, a great authentic drumlin of a man.

This account began in some North Monaghan fields with images of hunting, war and death. It ends in South Monaghan fields, with the hare at rest in a poem he entitled 'Peace':

> And sometimes I am sorry when the grass
> Is growing over the stones in quiet hollows
> And the cocksfoot leans across the rutted cartpass
> That I am not the voice of country fellows
> Who now are standing by some headland talking
> Of turnips and potatoes or young corn
> Of turf banks stripped for victory.
> Here peace is still hawking
> His coloured combs and scarves and beads of horn.
>
> Upon a headland by a whinny hedge
> A hare sits looking down a leaf-lapped furrow
> There's an old plough upside down on a weedy ridge
> And someone is shouldering home a saddle-harrow.
> Out of that childhood country what fools climb
> To fight with tyrants Love and Life and Time?

And what, in time, can this old fool hope for? That the Irish meaning of the word Ulster (*Ulad* – a tomb) become meaningless, that this little county become borderless and that all the children of this island become happily one and working here at last? Is that rhetoric, a foolish dream or prophetic? It can happen, it will happen. Enough. Spring has come early. I must go out now; I have trees to plant.

64 In the morning, Co. Derry

65 Man from the Bogside, Co. Derry

66 Foyle Hospice, Co. Derry

67 In the afternoon, Derry, Co. Derry

68 In the evening, Derry, Co. Derry

COUNTY DERRY

Seamus Heaney　　　　　Five Derry Glosses

Derry derives from the Irish word doire, *meaning an oak grove. The city is associated with Saint Colmcille, 'the dove of the church', who subsequently exiled himself to the island of Iona. The local place-name, Dirraghs, in the fifth poem, is probably another anglicisation of* doire. *The imagery of the third poem is taken from Frances Yates's* The Art of Memory.

Derry was *oak grove.* We believed in that
Like a mystery: the inked-in, thick-bunched,
Green and deckled light, the acorns and dead leaves

Had all been transubstantiated
Into a hill-town airiness, Derry's lilt
And pure *éclat* and quick unleavened song.

English or Irish? Transmuted place or name?
A mystery. But Derry Colmcille
Were the clear words of a beginning,

The dove, the thing itself and its white sign,
The scribe's illumination, the small boat,
The poem of exile and blindfolded love.

The River Foyle, the Roe, the quick Moyola.
The tense of water is continuous
Past or present? Something in you always

Re-entering its swim, riding or quelling
The very currents that it is comprised of,
Everything you accumulated ever

In river vigils at high college windows,
On gravel beds, or waist-deep in cow-parsley
On the banks of self at evening . . .

Lick of fear: the dead leaf borne in silence
Swifter (it seemed) than the water's passage.
Remembered flow the sky-dipped willows trailed in.

Memory as a building or a city,
Well lighted, well laid out, appointed with
Tableaux vivants and costumed effigies:

Statues in purple cloaks, or painted red,
Ones wearing crowns, ones smeared with mud or blood.
Ancient memory primers approved such

Loci et imagines, images
Impressed on sites, like seals impressed on wax,
So that mind's eye retained the heightened meaning.

And who is this in our haunted townscape staring
But the student of mnemonics and fresh murders,
Incredulous, abstracted, totting, sealing?

Seven years. The usual spellbound term.
The world dreamt through one long suspended gaze
At the shiny glamour and projections

Of a schoolroom wallmap. Shelvings, selvedges
Of blue on blue deepened out from strands,
Colour charts of contours and of soundings

Foretold the heavenly pigments, Atlantic turquoise
Swam immensely north. But green went deep
As the unconscious in *Bann Valley*,

Acre and *holding*, *right-of-way* and *roof*,
Where (landlocked, time-lagged, pent up in gutturals)
We glossed ourselves with earth tones and with leaf shades.

The Dirraghs were the fields of the nearly blessed.
Here the oak groves had been retranslated
Into a townland of bog oak and turf stacks

Where gaunt ones in their shirt sleeves dug and barrowed
Or stood alone at dusk out on a spread-field —
Apparitions now, yet active still,

Still territorial, sure of their ground
And interested, not knowing how far
The country of the souls has been pushed back,

How long the lark has stopped outside the Dirraghs
And only seems unstoppable to them
Caught like a far hill in a freak of sunshine.

72 Clare Island, Co. Mayo

73 Rock and grass, Co. Mayo

74 Clare Island, Atlantic Ocean and rain over Croagh Patrick Mountain, Co. Mayo

76 Co. Mayo

COUNTY MAYO

Michael Longley   A Mayo Sequence

I

I want my funeral to include this detour
Down the single street of a small market town,
On either side of the procession such names
As Philbin, O'Malley, MacNamara, Keane.
A reverent pause to let a herd of milkers pass
Will bring me face to face with grubby parsnips,
Cauliflowers that glitter after a sunshower,
Then hay rakes, broom handles, gas cylinders.
Reflected in the slow sequence of shop windows
I shall be part of the action when his wife
Draining the potatoes into a steamy sink
Calls to the butcher to get ready for dinner
And the publican descends to change a barrel.
From behind the one locked door for miles around
I shall prolong a detailed conversation
With the man in the concrete telephone kiosk
About where my funeral might be going next.

II

An inch above the horizon
Where the fields dip, Mercury
Seems to be reflecting Venus,
As though you were carrying
Through the gate a candle-flame
And shielding it with your hand
For fear it might be put out
By the wind or the distance.

III

All the washing on the line adds up to me alone.
When the cows go home and the golden plover calls
I bring it in, but leave pegged out at intervals
Dooaghtry Lake and David's Lake and Corragaun,
Gaps in the dunes, a sky-space for the lapwings
And the invisible whiteness of your underthings.

IV

I could find my way to either lake at this late hour
Sleepwalking after the night-alarms of whooper swans.
If I get to sleep, the otter I have been waiting for
Will surface in the estuary near the stepping stones.

V

He walks past my bedroom window carrying a spade.
That Joseph Murphy, father of four sets of twins,
Jockey, lover of horses, the gun club's secretary,
Should hide in his cottage a ledger full of poems
Is hardly surprising: consider his grandfather
Who beachcombed from the strand barrels and spars
And built the first velocipede in Tullabaun.
Out of an umbrella and old sheets he improvised
A parachute, launched himself from the byre roof
And after a brief flight was taken to hospital.
On home-made crutches and slipping all the tethers
Joseph Murphy's grandfather swings past my window.

VI

I had been waiting for the peregrine falcon
As a way of coming to terms with the silence,
As a way of getting closer to you – an idea
Above the *dooach*, downy whirlwinds, the wind's
Mother-of-pearl for instance, an eddy of bones.

Did the peregrine falcon when I was cycling
To meet you, swoop from the corner of my eye
And in and out of the culvert and out of sight
As though to avoid colliding with me – wings
Under the road, a blur of spokes and feathers?

VII

As though it were the only one in Ireland
I lie above Corragaun and watch an otter
Tying and untying knots in the undertow
And wiring me like a harebell to the wind.

VIII

I have hidden a key under the drystone wall
For lovers to make after me a home from home –
My gifts turf in a creel, buckets of lake water,
Their witnesses waders gathering for Greenland,
The Arctic, and pebbly nests below the snow-line.
I sleep on the other side of the hill from them.

79 Roonagh's Quay, Co. Mayo

IX

A wintry night, the hearth inhales
And the chimney becomes a windpipe
Fluffy with soot and thistledown,
A voice-box recalling animals:
The leveret come of age, snipe
At an angle, then the porpoises'
Demonstration of meaningless smiles.
Home is a hollow between the waves,
A clump of nettles, feathery winds,
And memory no longer than a day
When the animals come back to me
From the townland of Carrigskeewaun,
From a page lit by the Milky Way.

X

It begins in a boreen, a crush of fuchsia hedges.
One raven rolls in and out of the red wind.
Meadowsweet, loosestrife sway along the ditch
And wait to cross over at the end of my days.

81 Through the fields passing the Mweelra Mountains, Co. Mayo

82 Man with wheelbarrow, Longford, Co. Longford

COUNTY LONGFORD

Eilís Dillon

Longford is a quiet county. Water slides silently along in rivers or in the canal, or lies still in tree-lined lakes. In the summer air, gradually small sounds begin to fill the ear – the rustle of water in the tall rushes, the rattle of dead reeds against the pebbly shore, the chirp of water-hens, the strange grunting sound of swans in quiet conversation with each other, sometimes an unexplained swish of grasses where a small animal has passed close by.

Even the great river Shannon is quiet as it moves along the border of the county. Motor cruisers wind through the wooded fields, pausing in the locks on the Royal Canal, their engines ticking peacefully. This is where Goldsmith spent his early years, where from a little rise opposite his father's house he could see 'the most pleasing horizon in nature'.

The family moved a few miles away, into Westmeath, when Goldsmith was a child. The countryside is much the same there, and his nostalgia for his native places is powerfully expressed in 'The Deserted Village', especially when he writes of his longing to end his days there:

> And as a hare whom hounds and horn pursue
> Pants to the place from which at first she flew,
> I still had hopes, my long vexations pass'd,
> Here to return – and die at home at last.

He never did, and one regrets that he moved his famous Vicar of Wakefield to England, though his home was clearly that part of Ireland that Goldsmith knew so well. In fact the model for the vicar may well have been his father, who was certainly the model for the preacher in 'The Deserted Village':

> At church with meek and unaffected grace
> His looks adorned the venerable place;
> Truth from his lips prevailed with double sway,
> And fools, who came to scoff, remained to pray.

Though Goldsmith lamented the 'deserted village', Longford was a populous county in his day. Visiting it in 1776 Arthur Young commented on the fact that there was no emigration. He attributed this partly to the success of the linen-weaving: 'A gentleman unknown, giving £500 to be distributed to poor weavers in loans of £5 each' revitalised what had been a dead industry. All the poor people took to linen-spinning and the weavers prospered. But Young commented on the dreadful poverty, and he disapproved of the methods – or lack of methods – in agriculture. Mr Mahon of Ballymahon, the scene of Goldsmith's play *She Stoops to Conquer*, had five thousand acres of bog on the banks of the Shannon, 'all improvable'. But Young commends Mr Mahon's growth of trees and his planned hedging and ditching, which must have stood out in the bare countryside.

Maria Edgeworth saw no reason to transport her characters out of their native county. *Castle Rackrent* is firmly placed in Longford, though she does not say so, and she used her experience of her neighbours there to deliver her powerful message. Her father had seen his family's property in Ireland as a useful terrain in which to conduct his experiments in farming. It is interesting that he took his entire family to live there in 1782, when Ireland seemed about to realise its potential under a native government. Maria was then fifteen years old, but she had been taken to Edgeworthstown for two years at the age of six, after her father's second marriage. From the date of her second visit, Ireland was her home.

In 1798 the Edgeworths witnessed the disastrous effect of that saddest of all Irish risings, when gentry and strong farmers and the poor peasantry made a combined attempt to achieve control over their own affairs. The family had fled from their home at Edgeworthstown to Longford town, and Mr Edgeworth almost lost his life there when he was mistakenly thought by the loyalists to have supported the rebels.

Mr Edgeworth was an interesting man, one of the great reformers of the eighteenth century. An enthusiastic member of the Dublin Society for the Improvement of Husbandry – now the Royal Dublin Society – he invented farm machinery and ran a model estate. During the Napoleonic wars he offered to establish telegraphic communications of his own invention throughout the country but his offer was declined. He published details of his proposed apparatus in his 'Essay on the Art of conveying Swift and Secret Intelligence' in the sixth volume of the *Transactions of the Royal Irish Academy*, of which he was one of the founders.

Edgeworth married four times and was the father of eighteen children. This gave him the opportunity to test his theories of education, which more or less followed those of Rousseau and were far removed from the thinking of the time. Children should be constantly with their parents and should never be subjected to the corrupting influence of bad example. Thus their natural good nature and good sense would ensure that they would develop in virtue. Like his agricultural theories, this one was highly successful.

Her father had a strong influence on Maria, and her novel *The Absentee* probably expresses his thoughts on the immorality of failing to live and work on one's own estates. He is often blamed for siphoning off her talents into improving stories for small children, but these contain great natural vitality. Oddly enough, she never mentions religion as a source of virtue, and as a contemporary commentator said, '. . . she makes it appear unnecessary by exhibiting perfect virtue without it.' She and her father seem to have been entirely unaware of the existence of the ruined monasteries on the islands in Lough Ree, to us a mysterious and profound witness to the past glories of Ireland.

The same unawareness is true of Goldsmith. Both he and Maria Edgeworth came of planter stock which had never become 'more Irish than the Irish themselves'. Even in exile they retained something of the certainties of their powerful ancestors and in the case of the Edgeworths felt that they were naturally leaders of men. Perhaps because of their origins, they seem to have been precluded from touching the nerve-centre of the original Irish culture.

A third Longford writer, Padraic Colum, had no such difficulty. He managed to move freely between this world and that of ancient Irish mythology, with its life-sized fairy world superimposed on the real one. His children's book, *The King of Ireland's Son*, is the epitome of the true Irish folk-tale, a combination of kings and enchanters, talking animals and rural scenes and activities, all linking together several interconnected stories which are solved at the very end.

Colum's father was Master of the Workhouse in Longford town, and no doubt it often housed wandering story-tellers when times were hard. Padraic must have heard a great many stories before he was able to produce this masterpiece. There are no great battles nor struggles for power, just a gentle love story with obstacles, mostly magical, which must be overcome before the lovers can be united to live happily ever after. It finishes with two wedding feasts. At the first one:

> ... there were seven hundred guests at the short table, eight hundred at the long table, nine hundred at the round table, and a thousand in the great hall. I was there and I heard the whole story. But I got no present save shoes of paper and stockings of buttermilk and these a herdsman stole from me as I crossed the mountains.

At the second wedding:

> They had Greek honey and Lochlinn beer; ducks from Achill, apples from Emain and venison from the Hunting Hill; they had trout and grouse and plovers' eggs and a boar's head for every King in the company. And these were the Kings that sat down with the King of Eirinn: the King of Sorcha, the King of Hispania, the King of Lochlinn and the King of the Green Island who has Sunbeam for his daughter.

In spite of its tranquil appearance, Longford has had a violent history. Its most recent episode occurred during the War of Independence, when the notorious Black and Tans had vowed to burn systematically one Irish village after another. They began with Balbriggan, not far from Dublin, and met with no resistance. When they settled on their next target, Ballinalee, a few miles from Longford town, the local blacksmith, Seán MacEoin, organised a defence worthy of a professional soldier. He was entirely successful and the campaign of burnings was abandoned as a result.

In the last two centuries, famine and cholera took a large toll of the population, and emigration reduced it still further. Now, by the quiet shores of Lough Ree one may stand and see the dragon-flies dipping to drink, leaving a widening circle, or hear the brown trout leap with a splashing tail out of the water, or in the early morning see a stoat's funeral, the body carried in front and the mourning animals following in procession. A local naturalist claims that he saw this. If Padraic Colum had been passing by, he would have noticed that the leading stoat was carrying a magic gold ring in his mouth, and was willing to part with it for a good cause. One would probably have to be a king's son before the offer would be made but it would be worth anyone's while to try.

86 Man with ladder, Longford, Co. Longford

87 Man with cigarette, Longford, Co. Longford

88 Shopping I, Omagh, Co. Tyrone

COUNTY TYRONE

Benedict Kiely

Tyrone among the Bushes,
You're the finest spot I know.
To see again the winding Strule
A thousand miles I'd go.
The rugged Glens of Gortin
And dear old Bessy Bell...

Even the opening lines of Frank McCrory's popular song touch right away the heart of any Tyrone man, present landscapes to his eyes, and remind him too of much history.

Those bushes for instance would be most deep and leafy and luxuriant in, say, the Clogher Valley of South Tyrone, under the enchanted hill of Knockmany in the country of William Carleton (1794–1869) of the *Traits and Stories of the Irish Peasantry*, and of the poet John Montague who celebrates the place, and much more, in his work 'The Rough Field'.

The Strule winds north through rich lands associated with Lady Blessington and her noble lord. The rugged Glens of Gortin could include Glenlark where the great Hugh O'Neill, tradition says, drilled his pikemen to face the soldiers of the first Elizabeth.

The name of the mountain, Bessy Bell, mingles and confuses legends of the mythical Fianna and Fionn MacCumhaill with later renaming or misnaming of the mountain by the Hamiltons of Baronscourt, the Duke of Abercorn's people.

Or perhaps I should have said earlier: the heart of any man from West Tyrone. For one of the problems about Tyrone is that it is two counties. Having said so much I am forced to stop and rethink. For Tyrone is not, among the counties, the only sufferer in that respect. Take Tipperary, which may be more than two. Consider the length, the sheer length, of Roscommon from top to bottom, whichever is top or bottom (even in Roscommon they may not be quite in agreement about that). And as for Cork. And Kerry. And Mayo, God help us.

No, having said that Tyrone is two counties, East and West, I look at the map which I carry in my mind and see it shading itself off, still splendidly and varyingly coloured and in spite of the times it now suffers, into at least four counties, the Lough Shore, east on Lough Neagh, the Clogher Valley, the valleys of the Strule and the Mourne, and the great unifying centre which, like the boss on a shield, *is* the true heart of historic Ulster: the Sperrin Mountains.

If I were sending to Tyrone a friend who had never been there before, I would naturally send him first to my home town, Omagh, and to my friends therein, and after that, by Gortin and Plumbridge and Crannagh, into the Sperrins, along the Glenelly River, under the shadows of Sawel and Dart mountains to look in our legendary Glanconkyne where, after the fatal battle of Kinsale (1601), that great Hugh O'Neill, a fugitive on his native sod, thought his black thoughts. Then on to emerge, by Slieve Gallen Braes, renowned in a famous ballad, at Cookstown and on to the Lough Shore at the High Cross of Ardboe. My friend might be in great danger of being found trespassing in County Derry, or Londonderry, depending on your politics. But up in that chaste and lonely mountainland, county or other boundaries would not seem to be of much importance.

One spot in Omagh town my travelling friend must carefully avoid: the spot where the Comte d'Avaux turned back. This will be difficult for him to do, since nobody knows where exactly the spot is, or whether it is buried under stone or brick or tarmacadam or a three-hundred-year-old accumulation of clay. But there must be some odd enchantment about the spot where a king had his final tiff with the representative of another king, and that representative turned his back on Tyrone and Omagh and James Stuart, and off with him, home to France.

The Comte, there in Omagh town, was representing the Sun King and had the reputation for being a man of sense. But James Stuart, it was said, resented his high-handed ways, and James was, in all God's truth, high-handed enough himself. They had commenced the journey to the fatal walls of Derry. My authority here is Sir Charles Petrie:

> D'Avaux had not accompanied James to Derry. The King had gone by way of Armagh, Charlemont, Omagh and Strabane, but the ambassador had only followed him as far as Omagh, for he liked neither the purpose of the journey nor the discomfort involved.

For myself I like to think that the haughty couple parted company on the ancient hump of what is still known as the King's Bridge, at Crevenagh, over the Drumragh River before it enters the town to join the Camowen and form the Strule and to go on north to become the Mourne at Newtownstewart and to shape, though I say it, one of the loveliest river valleys in Ireland: good rivers to fish, too, and the home town has many expert fishermen.

> Thrice happy and blest were the days of my childhood,
> And happy the hours I wandered from school,
> By Mountjoy's green forest, our dear native wildwood
> And the green flowery banks of the serpentine Strule . . .

A verse, the first of several of a strange old ballad whose origins may go back to, say, 1815–20 when the slump in the timber trade that followed Waterloo and the peace drove the wood-rangers from the Blessington estates, along the river, to emigrate to the New World. The tradition is that they would mostly have been Irish-speakers from the glens of Sperrins from, say, Glenlark where in the 1930s there were still old people speaking native Irish. While the French wars were on, the axes of those men helped to keep Lord and Lady Blessington and Count D'Orsay gallivanting.

In the old Pratie Market, the location of which is still to be discovered but which is now forever devoid of praties, are the ghosts of men in homespun, speaking Irish, great axes on shoulders (for they never ventured forth without them), talking about the sea ahead of them and the fabled woods of Canada.

Where, at what is now Newtownstewart, the Dwenkillew River takes the Glenelly with it from the mountains to meet the Strule and make the Mourne, O'Neill crossed the water to go north into the mountains. There is a pool still called Buckety, which being interpreted could mean Hugh's whirlpool.

Two mountains, or two ladies, watch like goddesses over the rivers at that junction: Bessy Bell and Mary Gray, two ladies from the court of a Scottish king. They, like Boccaccio's ladies but not so well accompanied, fled the court to escape a plague and built a hut in the wildwood and thatched it over with rushes. They are mentioned in passing in Thomas Carlyle's *The French Revolution*. Two hills, in Stirlingshire I think, were called after them, and some of the Hamiltons of Baronscourt, riding out on their new land, named the Irish hills from a fancied resemblance to the Scottish hills.

But as my scholarly schoolfriend Brian MacBride of Newtownstewart may point out to you, there was an older name for the mountain now called Bessy Bell, that older name meaning the altars of Baal or Balor and sounding to a stranger's ear not unlike the name of the Scottish lady: so there may have been a double reason for her now presiding over that Ulster meeting of the waters.

Just as Sion Mills, further downstream, may take its name not from the heavenly Sion for which we all sigh but from the Irish Suidhe Fhionn, or the camping-place of Fionn MacCuinhaill and his mythological militia, the Fianna. Or Bessy Bell mountain may be that Sliabh Truim from which Fionn and his companions set forth to hunt for a day all across the countryside, now the full width of the County Tyrone, and to camp that night on the shore of the great lake.

To come to more recent times.

We are indebted to two men for making the approach to and the knowledge of the Sperrins more easy and more attainable. They are Tom Ballantine and William Todd who, on behalf of the Sperrin Tourist Development Association, prepared an illustrated booklet called *The Sperrins: A Hidden Beauty*. All the basic information is in these pages. The booklet was printed by the *Tyrone Constitution* in Omagh, and I take the liberty of borrowing from the introduction:

> A range of mountains heavily draped in heather and presenting glorious pageants of colour at the various seasons of the year. Spreading in bold contour across Ulster, from the border of Donegal in the west to near the shores of Lough Neagh in the east, forming a boundary between Londonderry and Tyrone. An area of ever-changing scenery, high uplands, vast domes against the sky, lush green valleys, forests, dark hidden loughs and bright streams rushing over clear rocks.

The map that makes up the centrepiece of the booklet wisely does not confine itself strictly to the mountainous area, nor exactly within the county boundary. The Englishmen who shired Ireland and, for that matter, the chieftains and clans who went before them were not always regardful of natural boundaries: and this map sensibly spills over a little into Donegal and Fermanagh and a lot into Derry.

But draw a line from that most historic town of Dungannon, of O'Neill and of the Volunteers of 1782, to Ballygawley, to Petigo, to Strabane, to Donemana, to Dungiven, to Toome and back to Dungannon, and you have enclosed a most interesting area of brown land and green land, lakelands and river valley. And you may meditate on what the great O'Neill was fighting for and about. And hope that peace may come to camp for ever in those ancient places and preserve what Walter Scott called 'all the glory of Tyrone'.

93 Shopping II, Omagh, Co. Tyrone

94 In the tannery, Carlow, Co. Carlow

COUNTY CARLOW

Frank McGuinness

Where I come from in Donegal is called Inishowen, which translates as 'John's Island'. But it is a peninsula, not an island. Inishowen is bordered by Lough Foyle and Lough Swilly, the lake of shadows. These loughs are not lakes but fjords. Our place-names bear the mark of invention. I like them for that linguistic reason. Carlow means 'the four lakes'. You search the county in vain for them: they have long disappeared. Yet water is the basis for all my images of Carlow, for the River Barrow seems to flow everywhere through it, and all the land is arable. I first visited Carlow for a wedding. Fertility was in the air. The walk between Bagenalstown and Royal Oak along the banks of the Barrow bloomed that year with rhododendrons, and in my memory, that Sunday we walked there the world turned pink with pleasure.

A city of granite, Carlow town houses fifteen thousand people. The bedrock of the Wicklow Mountains crosses through to the county. The Norman castle is now a shell. It has its power but it is not the most haunting elegy to Carlow's past. In the town there is a mass grave, wherein lie the remains of the croppies, massacred in 1798, more than two hundred dead in a day. To my generation, the croppies suggest only the sickeningly sentimental song *The Croppy Boy*. But that grave in Carlow moved me, linked as it is to the tombs of the dead, unknown, unremembered, shades without shape, falling defenceless in all world wars.

The Protestant community survives in Carlow. Bagenalstown has a thriving Church of Ireland. In this respect the town differs markedly from the rest of the midlands and deep south of Ireland. The town itself dates from 1780, planned by a descendant of the Elizabethan gurrier, Marshall Bagenal, who lost the Battle of the Yellow Ford to Hugh O'Neill. (Keep it quiet we won that one, why spoil a perfect record?) Bagenalstown was envisaged as a new Versailles, a town naturally divided by the Barrow. The plan was scuppered. The court-house now stands with its back to the town. I approve of defiant architecture. The great stretch of empire touched Bagnelstown practically and the smell of Indian jute soaked Brown's mill. Up until the 1960s the children of Bagenalstown queued each Christmas for the sixpence bestowed to the populace by Mrs Brown. They still would, I suppose.

John Betjeman lamented that the small towns of Ireland were neglected by poets, and honoured Dungarvan, 'Dungarvan in the rain', in the great poem 'The Irish Unionist's Farewell to Great Hellstrom in 1922'. The midlands of Ireland are likewise neglected. I only went to Carlow for reasons of the heart. I didn't leave mine there. But the county has a peace about it that defines it, and its landscape is mighty by reason of its modesty. Protecting the county is Brown's Dolmen, the biggest in Ireland, and its strange strength typifies the place. I like Carlow for it doesn't look to be noticed. Quiet places, like quiet men, have a lot going for them.

96 Selling oil, Co. Offaly

COUNTY OFFALY

Emma Cooke

It is a lovely place, especially in late summer when the air wafting in from the bog tastes sweet as an apple. The towns are sleepy, with streets stretching out like tired elastic and big market squares. The older houses are huge, with zigzag corridors, hide-and-seek cubby-holes and acres of attics. Between the latest fast food take-aways and video amusement dens dark-painted shops and pubs remain with windows full of gewgaws and cornflakes boxes faded by daylight. The countryside itself is flat as can be, wide well-tilled fields, rambling prosperous farms, cottages with their windows stuffed with plants and their gardens tight-packed with flowers and vegetables. The wide grey towers of the generating stations fuelled by peat from the bogs loom over the landscape, monuments to a certain stage of economic development.

There are other monuments – Clonmacnoise, Birr Castle, the Cistercian Abbey near Roscrea – but because of its flatness, and the denseness of its woods and screening hedges, a great deal of Offaly remains hidden from the casual passer-by. You have to be a native to press your hand against one of the heavy hall doors and push. Inside you have the big hall, flagged floor, a fireplace as an open joke against the draughts and, closing the door behind you, you find yourself in a pale grey fanlit dusk.

Most of the principal rooms of these big midland town houses remain unused, or have been taken over for storage by the adjoining family business. Instead the occupants themselves are tucked cosily in a small back sitting-room. There are old copies of *The Lady* and *Woman's Weekly* on an occasional table. Framed wedding photographs jostle each other along the top of a piano – your grandparents, your parents, your brothers, your sisters, your own. You lift the piano-lid and play middle C. It reverberates with the same cold splash you felt dipping your toe into the River Barrow on the first day of summer long ago. But nobody swims in the River Barrow now; and the fish are disappearing from it too. And from the other swimming-places because of bad anti-pollution laws and people who don't care.

The River Barrow is the dividing line between Leix and Offaly for the town of Portarlington. I was born on the Offaly side. On evenings after inter-county hurling or football matches the place splits into two camps – our Offaly end and the enemy. Next day it is forgotten. A highlight of any local festival is a tug of war between Offaly and Leix, teams pulling from opposite banks.

Because the county is so flat, one of the best ways to see it all is on a bicycle. 'Where else could you go up a hill down?' we shout on the bouncy road to Geashill where the bike gathers enough momentum on the downward slope to carry you up to the top of the next hill. Or you can take it easy and pedal to Edenderry to admire the pretty square and the canal. Or you can pack a picnic and take one of the hidden, curving lanes that lead out to the heart of the bog and munch sardine sandwiches while you admire the heather and the bog-cotton and listen for the different bird-cries. But you must get home early. People have been drowned on the high bog after dark, have fallen into bog-holes and not been found for months.

There are ghost stories and legends about the high bog that make it too spooky for night-time excursions. You can push a stick down a hole in a certain spot guarded by a leafless tree and rattle it against a coffin. Nobody knows whose it is but it's there, intact, preserved by the bog which keeps everything. Butter from hundreds of years back has been dug up fresh and sweet as the day it was made by some long vanished *bean a ti*.

The big gentlemen's houses of Offaly, owned by merchants and wealthy farmers, were not built near the bog. They were built on the outskirts of towns, or surrounded by the best arable land. During the 1920s and 30s, two decades of civil and economic trouble, many of them handed up their treasures – not into a peaty vault, but into the hands of the highest bidder.

The trend has continued: auction fever is still a midland complaint. I was infected as a child, watching my father bid for a suit of armour in a castle outside Tullamore, running a nervous finger along the backs of gilt chairs of French origin bought by my grandfather, exploring the intricacies of a labyrinthine work-box made by a Huguenot cabinet-maker.

The word 'refugee' was first used to describe these French people forced to flee to another country to escape religious persecution. Many of them found peace and welcome in Offaly. Maybe that's part of our auction fever. The willingness to give a good home to something which nobody else wants, combined with a hard-headed desire to acquire something valuable for practically nothing.

Of course there are more modern houses nowadays, council housing, trendy bungalows, new estates like they have everywhere else. And central heating, the latest plumbing, less room for old sofas, less wall-space for big tapestries, the wrong settings for faded damask. Much of the Offaly I grew up with has been siphoned away, people and things, to different pastures. White paint, chipboard, formica, jazzy tiling beat upon the eye. But the local card players still play 'twenty-five' and the ceilidh bands are still as good, and if you're not light on your feet you might as well stay at home. And people still sit up until all hours of the night. It has something to do with the heaviness of the air, which lightens after dark so that you suddenly wake up just before midnight. If you're not a card player or a dancer and the telly has gone off then all you can do is read a book. Blockbusters are the most popular mode of fiction in Offaly. Anything under five hundred pages is hard to sell.

'Don't start just coming up for funerals,' an Offaly cousin said to me recently. As I drove home I carried a recollection of locked rooms, empty sheds roofed with red galvanised iron, ladies having tea-parties under sun umbrellas, cobble-stoned yards, weeds in corners and moss fingering brick walls. Some weeks later, as I was driving to Dublin from County Clare, a roadside sign saying 'Welcome to Offaly' flashed across my vision. I was back, only for a mile or two, but I was back. All I had to do was turn left and I could travel on right up through the old familiar heart of it again. It was a happy thought, bright as an apple blossom, a talisman for my journey.

99 Man in bar, Co. Offaly

100 Woman shopping, Co. Roscommon

COUNTY ROSCOMMON

Christopher Fitz-Simon

Once upon a time it befell Ailill and Medb that, when their royal bed had been prepared for them in Rath Cruachain in Connacht, they spoke together as they lay on their pillow, 'In truth, woman,' said Ailill, 'she is a well-off woman who is the wife of a nobleman.' 'She is indeed,' said the woman. 'Why do you think so?' 'I think so,' said Ailill, 'because you are better off today than when I married you.' 'I was well-off before "marrying" you,' said Medb.

This laconic exchange between Queen Medb and her husband Ailill took place at Rath Cruachan, which is right in the centre of Roscommon, a county which is right in the centre of Ireland, two thousand years ago – give or take a century or two. Their forts and enclosures (some would call them 'palaces', others of more scientific inclination would refer to 'settlements') cover two square miles of intersecting walls, ditches and earthen circles. One of the entrances to the underworld is here; and there is a cumbrous monolith which marks the grave of Dathaí, last pagan king of Ireland, who was struck by lightning when attempting to cross the Alps in a chariot – his remains were carried home by a faithful postillion. It is a strange, expansive place, on a high grassy plateau, and it was from here that Medb set out with her warriors on her quest for the brown bull of Cooley, as related in the *Táin Bó Cúailnge*, the central saga of the Ulster Cycle and the earliest vernacular epic in western literature, which was passed down by word of mouth till transcribed in the eighth century. Many poets have made versions of it since that time.

Not far away, at Castlestrange, there is a granite boulder – granite is a curiosity in Roscommon – incised with curvilinear ornaments in the La Tène style; nobody knows whence it came, but it is far from fanciful to relate it to the culture of Medb's time, and certainly its convoluted patterns bear quite a canny resemblance to the deviousness of that queen's mind. The pungent, ironic periods of the *Táin* and the quirky spirals of Castlestrange speak with one voice, and are a thousand times more majestic and confident than the poetry which disclosed itself at the end of the nineteenth century to Douglas Hyde – folklorist, scholar and first President of Ireland – in the barony of Ballintubber some thirty miles to the north. That it disclosed itself at all is quite remarkable, for by that time the ancient Gaelic culture had all but vanished under the influence of foreign settlers from across the sea.

Today the eye lights unsparingly on images of decay and death: of privation, of cruelty, of defeat. All around the county we come across scattered remnants of monuments raised by the people of civilisations which, lacking the strength for survival, ended here among the cropped grass and sparse heather. A stone inscribed by a sophisticated hand centuries before Ptolemy put a hesitant name on this place; a portentous rock where kings were crowned; the shell of a quadrangular castle with bulging bastions; a roofless Romanesque nave; fragments of scrolled capitals among the nettles recalling a new grandeur imposed by colonists who had read of Ionia in the pattern-books of the eighteenth century. The message of failure to flourish, to progress, even to settle, is stencilled on the drystone face of every bitter townland.

The Roscommon terrain undulates without much interruption from the low-lying meadows of the Shannon and Suck to the only marginally more elevated Plains of Boyle in the north of the county. The mountains which rise abruptly above this beech-sequestered little town bear a topographical affinity to neighbouring Sligo. If I had been drawing the boundaries for Sir Henry Sidney in 1585 I would have made Roscommon end more ceremoniously, at the Boyle River which links Lough Gara to Lough Key; but the cartographers employed during the Tudor conquest had more pressing matters on their minds — matters relative to the distribution of land which was not properly theirs to distribute, matters of dire rivalry between newly planted families, and the supreme difficulty concerning the vanquished natives of the place who were forever gathering in grim expectation of repossession.

Henry VIII and his two daughters were by no means the first to select and parcel Roscommon land for distribution to favoured henchmen. Henry III had included almost the whole of what is now the county in a grant made to Richard de Burgo. By the end of Elizabeth I's reign the native septs had, willy-nilly, re-established themselves, and it was left to Oliver Cromwell's crew-cut entrepreneurs to repackage the land for the betterment of the English and Scottish adventurers who followed them on their campaign of devastation. The O'Conor Don is said to have been the only head of a Roscommon clan to regain any significant portion of his property after the restoration of Charles II (over there in distant London) and this he did by sleight of hand, a gesture which encompassed forelock-touching of so prodigious a nature that it resembled semaphore.

Clonalis has been the seat of the O'Conors for two millennia. The important point, of course, is that it is there, home of a great Roman Catholic landed family. Almost all the great houses built by Protestant planter families — who perhaps possessed a more keenly-developed sense of visual decorum — have disappeared.

The handsome gate piers of the planter mansions remain: but what use is a gate which leads to nowhere save a rushy field where once a carriage drive led through parkland to a fine façade? The splendid classical arch designed to frame an avenue of hardwoods at Mote Park now opens directly onto a forest of Christmas trees planted in rows by the modern State after the lands had been taken over. Another gateway, that of French Park, has been purchased by connoisseurs and set up in prosperous Kildare where the preservation of Georgiana has become a cult and fine masonry is respected for its design and craftsmanship and is not confused with the political provenance of those who ordained it.

Of French Park itself nothing remains but the tumbling estate walls. It was a three-storey house with flanking pavilions, designed by Richard Castle (author of Leinster House, Dublin; now Dáil Eireann) in the early eighteenth century. Douglas Hyde descended from the Frenches on his mother's side. He grew up in the village of Frenchpark where his father was the Protestant rector. Therein lies one of the most extraordinary tales of what we are pleased to call the cross-fertilisation of cultures, a tale which, in the telling, changed the course of modern Irish literature.

French Park has gone. So have Ballinagare and Castlerea. Wander where you will, the stone skeletons catch the passing glance through rank shrubberies and gappy fences. Palladian Mount Talbot, châteauesque Kilronan, neo-classical Mantua. Of Clooneyquin

103 Buying shoes, Co. Roscommon

(birthplace of Percy French, the watercolourist and song-writer), Runnamoat and Rockville not a rib of roof remains. Only curious confabulations of ornamental trees — copper-beech, cedar of Lebanon, monkey-puzzle — on the edge of an alder-fringed lake or in view of some broad bend of river, show where a mansion once stood; and half a mile away by the tarmacadamed road is the inescapable, ubiquitous gateway with its quaint empty lodge.

Roscommon's most famous, and most imposing, house was Rockingham, once the home of the Stafford-King-Harmons (no Gaelic syllables in that hyphenation). Nash designed it, and adorned it with two dozen Ionic columns. Like several of its neighbours in the well-watered, almost luxuriant territory of Boyle, Rockingham provided employment for dozens of labourers, groundsmen, gardeners, stable-boys, footmen, housemaids and kitchen-maids. There was a tunnel leading from the basement to the shore of Lough Key; its debouchment beside a little jetty was discreetly screened by rhododendrons and magnolia so that the servants, unloading the turf which was transported by boat across the lake to stoke the household fires, could not be observed from the drawing-room windows. Even a picturesque peasant was unwelcome in the background of this idyllic landscape.

It is not true that most of the now-derelict country houses were razed during the 'troubles' of 1922–23; a small proportion were, but the majority simply fell into decay due to the neglect of their owners, many of whom just 'went away', selling the land — which could fetch a good price; but nobody, except the odd order of nuns, wanted to maintain big draughty buildings. Some estates were bought by 'farmers', who dismantled the buildings for whatever they could get for the slates and the lead. Some of the retreating ascendancy families may have been 'improving landlords' in their day, but the unpalatable fact is that most were not, and when the latter moved out to Woking and Torquay, to the delight of their erstwhile tenants, and the Irish Land Commission divided up the properties into smallholdings, many of the newly liberated found that they had been better off when in service to the gentry, who had at least provided continuity of employment.

The landlords who spent the shillings and pence ground out of an alien peasantry on the education of their sons at Eton and Wellington, on seasons in Dublin, London and the spas of Europe if their livers were complaining, and who drank themselves unconscious on wine imported through Galway from Bordeaux and Hamburg, belonged to Horseback Hill rather than to Heartbreak House. The poets, playwrights, novelists, painters, and those artistic wasters romantically referred to as dreamers, who grew up in the Anglo-Irish Protestant tradition, more typically came from families situated in the various gradations of the middle class.

In spite of his great-great-grandmother being a member of the French family, Douglas Hyde's people were mainly scholastic and clerical. When he was a boy in north Roscommon the country people were still largely Irish-speaking, though the educational system of the day saw to it that they would not be so for much longer. Children were provided with a stick which was hung round their necks and upon which parents were supposed to cut a notch for every Gaelic word uttered; next day the schoolteacher administered the same number of strokes of the cane.

105 Man in bar, Co. Roscommon

Hyde, as was the practice among Protestant families living in remote places, received his early education in the home. His father taught him Greek, Latin and arithmetic; his unofficial, and by far the most influential, teachers were an old man called Johnny Lavan who told him stories in Irish, Seumas O'Hart, who also had a rich store of folk-tales, and Martin O'Brennan, who mowed the Rectory lawn and conversed with Hyde in Irish on all manner of topics; it was a sign of the times that O'Brennan's daughter, who was the Hydes' housemaid, could not speak any Irish at all. By the time he was sent to school in Dublin at the age of thirteen, Hyde had filled notebooks with poems and stories written out phonetically – for he had no means of learning the Gaelic script or spelling. One of the poems which he noted down in this uncouth style turned out to be Antoine O Reachtabhraigh's 'Cill Aodáin', which had been circulated, like all the rest of that poet's work, orally. 'Cill Aodáin' is now in every Irish school anthology and has been translated into English by several modern writers, among them Frank O'Connor and Brendan Kennelly, and Raftery has been reinstated in Ireland's pantheon of poets.

Illness sent Hyde back to Roscommon after only one term at school, and he dedicated himself to the systematic collection of Irish folk literature. After an extraordinarily brilliant university career, and a period as a lecturer abroad, he returned to Ireland in 1891 and devoted the rest of his life to the study and revival of the Irish language. In 1893 he founded the Gaelic League, and also published *Love Songs of Connacht*. Yeats, Lady Gregory and Synge pored over this remarkable volume. There had been many translations of Irish poetry and folk-tales made over the past hundred years, usually in rough ballad form or more politely influenced by Tennyson and Macaulay. Hyde said that he 'endeavoured to reproduce the vowel rythms as well as the exact metres of the original Irish poems'. Astonishing as it may now seem, *Love Songs of Connacht* was the earliest book which introduced the poetry of the Irish country people to those in Ireland who could not speak Irish themselves.

Hyde's aim had been, quite simply, to save the Irish language from extermination. In succeeding, he also created a powerful new literary form in English, a form of remarkable flexibility which made colourful use of Gaelic metaphor and the thought-process of the Gaelic people. The results rocked the foundations of the English-language drama, prose fiction and poetry as practised by Irish-born writers. The traditions, the deeper thoughts and aspirations of a people who, over the centuries, had become enslaved and who had seen their plutocratic culture deteriorate to the point where it existed only among the peasantry, had been reaffirmed and reinstated by one whose forebears were not of their race, and whose religion – for religion was the gauge by which such things were measured – was that of the usurper. Later, in gratitude, the people of Ireland elected Douglas Hyde as their President, and by subscription bought him a house at Ratra, between Lough Gara and Frenchpark, to which he retired. His grave is in the local churchyard, and the little limestone church is dedicated to his memory.

The speaking of Irish in the cottages around Frenchpark and Ballaghadereen and Ballinlough is no longer regarded as a crime, though not many, unfortunately, use the language outside the classroom. Rockingham House is gone, accidentally burned down in 1957, but its grounds are decently maintained by the Irish Forest and Wildlife Service as a public park, and on summer afternoons hundreds come to enjoy the view and the boating on Lough Key.

The guidebooks mention how the *Annals of Lough Key* came to be compiled there in the sixteenth century, and how the beautiful Una Bhán McDermott died for the love of the poet Tomás Láidir Coisdealbhach, and how two ash trees grew out of their graves and intertwined their branches. Douglas Hyde translated the poem 'Una Bhán', and, on account of his diligence and sensitivity, we are now able to share what for many years had been flowing under the ground, like the waters of the *turloughs*, or disappearing lakes, which are to be found in this limestone region.

Uisce fé thalamh (water beneath the land) is a local phrase normally used to denote rumour, or something which can only be discussed covertly. Ireland, her resplendent past and her secret hopes for a future free from the yoke of the foreigner, was the principal subject discussed in this way in the windy hedgerows and by firelight throughout the bleak seventeenth, eighteenth and nineteenth centuries. The poets of those times saw their country as a shining vision of a young woman, Roisín Dubh or Cáit ní Dhuibhir or called by many other names which cloaked her identity in symbol. When, out of despair and defeat, they had ceased to write of her in their own language, a young descendant of the same foreigner gave them a new voice in Roscommon, and they are now heard again throughout the length and breadth of Ireland.

> She is my store, oh, she my store,
> Whose grey eyes wounded me so sore,
> Who will not place in mine her palm,
> Nor love, nor calm me any more ...
>
> She's my desire, oh, my desire,
> She warms me like the bright sun's fire;
> Who were than wind-blown ice more cold,
> Were I so bold as to sit by her.

108 East Belfast, Co. Down

COUNTY DOWN

Medbh McGuckian

On the road-map County Antrim is pale green, with the wide inky carve and curve of the motorway. The motorway avoids the pale yellow of County Down, arteried by thin and fat scarlet veins, blue letters for mountains, black for towns. If you cut out the shapes of them and folded them over each other along the line from Belfast to Lough Neagh, you would have it in a nutshell, the wings of my soul, the open book of my heart and the male and female lungs of me, the hinges of my being, my Down and Connor diocese. Whoever has drawn their points and edges has drawn me, in me the Ards Peninsula fits exactly the glove of Island Magee, Coleraine beats against Newry like a butterfly, Rathlin where I have never been is the bright expansion and mirror of the tiny Guns Island you could wade out to from Ballyhornan.

Perhaps because it is an old map with Sellotape on the seams, and only the roads, not rainfall, vegetation, politics, geology, population, industry, language or religion, I feel in myself the Sellotaping of all Ireland, the cold eye of its segments on each other, how the major lough is a microcosm of a drowned land from which I burst separate away like breasts, a dove, a swimmer's arms, a plane. Derek Mahon quotes John Ardagh: 'If you cease to be seen and heard, if you go to live and work quietly in the provinces, then (unless your talent is exceptional) you cease to exist.' Have I waited here so long, too long, that Belfast is my propeller, my engine, fuel and wind? That is how, looking down on myself from this height, I appear to me.

Today, Boxing Day, St Stephen's Day (all days have two names), we drove down through Carryduff, Saintfield, Crossgar and Strangford to have scampi in Portaferry with Anne Devlin and her family. It was Ireland, day, a woman and dry going there. Coming back was England, through Kircubbin, past Carrowdore and Newtownards, night, wet and a man, a courageous road right alongside the lough coast, like the Antrim road that only loses its sea-nerve finally at Cushendall. I like that in it and the gingerbread villages, but it is not part of my scrapbook, it is for when you have nothing more to say, and the Waves of Troy are breaking on Helen's Bay:

> The sky is tall as over a runway,
> The land without marks so you will not arrive
>
> But pass through, though always skirting landfall.

I have passed through, eaten and shopped in Hillsborough and Ballynahinch. I have slept in Newcastle and walked in Castlewellan and Tullymore Park. But I have only ever lived, at the beginning of my two lives, in and around Downpatrick, that ancient seat, that feminine depression or lowland my car will now do anything to skirt. Until I was seven and reached the use of reason, it held all that I desired. Thirty years later it is the last place I seek, yet still the mould, womb and firer of my earliest, deepest and latest loves, my loves-till-death. It is my Lear's heath, where he found his reason and lost it.

I call it feminine because it is my mother and her mother and my motherhood. Although her people came from the Lough Shores near Randalstown, there was no retreat to any rural homestead in that direction. They always headed south – perhaps the buses were handier or cheaper. I was born before my time in August rather than September because that summer they had gone to Omeath, and my mother says the sea air brings it on. All the summers of my infancy they took a two-roomed half of a tin-roofed cottage at the end of a lane of such houses, in a then-unspoiled fishing *clachan* just about as far out of Downpatrick as Donaghadee from Bangor in the song. If there was no visiting priest my grandmother would walk those miles fasting to Sunday Mass, regardless of the weather or her bunions. Next door Vera played the current hits on her radio day and night. But what I found most strange was the way the road down by the rocks just melted away, into a stone wall, which haunted me like the witch's dissolution in *The Wizard of Oz*.

Now it is all caravans and cars. Then it was a flat, semi-militarised zone, with an airfield close by at Bishopscourt, prefabricated Army quarters behind a high fence, a Triffid-like atmosphere full of presentiment of the long occupation still to come. There were barbed-wire barricades on the shoreline from the war, at Killard a bleak radar station twisted remorselessly, cemented into a standing-stone. We saw U-boats on the horizon like Woody Allen, found grenades and unexploded bombs in the still-mined sand. No Remembrance Day brought into association in my mind red flowers and dead soldiers; my sister and I were no higher than the intensely crimson petals of the abundant poppies spotting the roadside, when a khaki-coloured jeep hurtled over us into the grass, and two young men lay under it.

One year my father's arms saved me from drowning, one year we could not swim because of the typhoid, and another year my sister and I were Goneril and Regan, swinging our smaller sister till she fell and injured an arm, and my mother turned away her face till we reached Downpatrick Hospital. That autumn when we all developed polio the arm would not heal, and everything was frozen like that. My malignant streak was confirmed the year they held a birthday party for me, since it was too rainy to go for the usual picnic to the wreck, and I was discovered charging my guests twopence to come in, if they had no present. Once when I was given sixpence for a skinned knee I ate a whole Fry's Chocolate Cream bar in secret myself. I felt so bad I knew I must be nearly at the age of the use of reason.

When we played house the other girls had romantic, filmy names, like Joyce-Ann, Ann-Jane, Mary Dorothy or Monica who rhymed with America and sang *The Black Hills of Dakota*. She showed me America behind Guns Island, the word repeated its beauty to me through hers. The last season we spent there I must have attained reasonableness, or the first awareness of the apple hanging on the tree of good and evil. The flies crusted thick on the streamers suspended from the ceiling, and my grandmother had to dab our sunburned backs all night with buttermilk that also formed a white coat, and on my birthday my brother and sister went out in a boat to the Copeland Islands and had knickerbocker glories, which I understood as divine vengeance, or the beginning of wisdom.

There was something equally sinister in the fascination that compelled me back subtly as the air of Omeath twenty years later. Someone who had reached the use of reason in Ballymena but preferred to commute from a bungalow in Downpatrick seemed only too grotesquely to reconcile most of my opposites in himself. Our first meeting was a stormy excursion along Ardglass Golf Course where his coat billowed like a sail or a presage. I wrote an incipient poem about the lopped captain's chair and body-thick rope he trailed Christ-like the length of Tyrella beach. There was no resisting the conviction that if called upon he too would sacrifice his night to one's back.

For three years we hovered around the Quoile Estuary and the Racecourse, but, as John Ardagh says, nothing will come of nothing in your own back yard, and our first child was not conceived until we spent the weekend in Killiney. There followed an idyllic nine months of newly-purchased fishing tackle and a Fiat Amigo dormobile for the future summers of the ménage à trois. I refused to hear of a Royal Victoria delivery, he must be born to the echo of Struell Wells in the shade of the cathedral with the bones of Patrick, Brigid and Colmcille, bells drifting from Inch Abbey and Loughinisland. But the institution that took things in hand turned out to be the gaol-house – I think of it all now in terms of fortifications and police stations. I discovered no fortress within myself, and had not dreamed that standing up after a birth was more difficult than standing up after polio.

One night about six weeks later I felt a funeral in my brain and my eyes would not close, a fly buzzed and I knew I would have to return to my father's house or drown. The hedgerow flowers were as bright as my childhood poppies, which was wrong. I could not sleep in Ballymena nor on the Antrim road, my child was Christ and the radio was God. They had just opened a cinema and a new swimming-pool, but the river had stolen my voice, and I sold my strawberry house with its strawberry bathroom. Our labrador pup had been run over because we had no gate, and I needed a gate as powerful as the gates of Castleward and Mount Stewart. But when snow covers the Mournes I remember sunburn, and on my mother's wall is a water-colour of a road that is beautiful because and although it leads nowhere.

There are believed to be between 10,000 and
12,000 children under 15 years of age suffering
from chronic juvenile polyarthritis or Stills Disease
as it is more commonly known
The Lady Hoare Trust which looks after many
physically disabled children
IS PARTICULARLY INTERESTED in the children
suffering from STILLS DISEASE and their families,
AND is also helping them in Hospital
The profits from this shop will go to help both
of these Trusts

113 Cinderella, Newtownards, Co. Down

114 In a small bar in Co. Waterford, demolished in late 1988

COUNTY WATERFORD

Peter Sirr

I don't, I think, have a strong sense of rootedness in particular locations and so, when place enters my poems, it's a bit shadowy, a bit foggy – even if minutely particularised. More often than not I tend to write about not being somewhere, or of stalking about ghost-like through landscapes and cityscapes, failing to scare anybody, failing to do more than register everything and hope some of the details add up. The poem which follows, then, is at least as much about not being in Waterford as about being there.

Less fancifully, the poem is an act of burglary carried out on my childhood (I lived in Waterford until I was nine) with proper names and authentic details thrown in to create the illusion of place. I think of remembering as a stealthy, burglarish process, and also, to complicate things further, I preoccupy myself here as much with what I fail to remember, or never knew, as with what I have retained. I hope the poem itself mimics some of the stealth and suspiciousness of the enterprise.

Breaking into Newtown Road

Stashed in the garden
with my notebook and binoculars

I case the house, observing
its comings and goings, its show of lights

its careless treasures
no one remembers.

I have come back for this
I have shinnied up the long black pipe

and gently, not a sound, lifted
the kitchen window, eased

the door, a crack, a hairline fracture
in which my father lights

one of the five cigarettes
he allows himself, and my mother

has poured them both a drink.
It is late, the children are asleep

no one else is here.
I have come back for this

I come here every night
holding a mike to the thread of light

in which my parents live.
Ten years of conversation

of smoke rings and silences
tenderness and argument

of watching TV, or doing nothing
of scattering the evidence

I creep around in the small hours
to assemble, pilfering

a packet of Sweet Afton
a ball of wool, handkerchiefs

and hairpins, a postcard
from Tramore, a corner

of the *News and Star* – everything held and relished
before I stuff it in my bag.

Ten years they live here, blow-ins
in the tight city

of my childhood. The house collapses
in the back of my mind

every night I reach my fingers towards their lives
and miss.

117 Waterford Sunday morning

118 Woman singing 'The Soldier's Song', Co. Waterford

COUNTY LOUTH

Maeve Kelly

When I was five years old my father bundled myself and my mother and brothers and sisters into a large black taxi and we drove across Ireland from Ennis in County Clare to his home town of Dundalk in County Louth. It was a wild March day in which clouds scudded across immense skies and showers challenged our magic carpet with scatters of hailstones. It was an awesome journey for us, travelling from our little nest in the West to unknown border territory. We had no idea why we were going or what we were going to, but we excelled ourselves by being more than usually carsick. My memory of the journey, apart from the drama of clouds seen through moving panes of glass, is of an odyssey punctuated by cries of 'Quick, quick, I want to be sick,' and of the potty in the back seat being produced so that we might ease our anguish without inconveniencing our driver with too many stops. Every now and again my mother announced that she must discard the contents of the potty and he would oblige her by pulling up to the still-leafless hedges where she refurbished our life-saving utensil. We successfully polluted the ancient hedgerows of Ireland with the contents of our poor little stomachs, groaning horribly as we did so and leaning for comfort against our mother and each other.

Every now and again, from the superior position of the front passenger seat, my father would turn his head and look at us in amazement before thankfully disengaging himself from our misery to carry on smoking his pipe and conversing sagely about national affairs with the driver. My mother got on with her woman's business of tending the wounded.

That journey is my first memory of the town where I grew up. Years later when I married and was farming in County Clare I often thought of our exodus from the county to which I had circuitously returned, of the wild cloudy March skies on the way, changing their shapes and colours, of the little towns appearing and disappearing, of the endless succession of hedgerows (which served such a useful purpose), of the lights of a big city and later the smaller lights of Dundalk. Sleepy-eyed and exhausted we blinked out of our transporter into a new life, ushered into it by the welcoming squeezes and hugs of a family friend who had lit fires and made beds and polished the house up but whose kisses filled our ungrateful hearts with rage and embarrassment.

My father was born on a farm near the racecourse in Dundalk. He hoped to inherit the land so that he could pass it on to us. He had worked it before leaving for other horizons. He did law-clerking and auctioneering at various periods of his life but never did get back to the land. His father left the place to whichever of his remaining sons could afford to pay his debts. With little money and five children to rear, my father was effectively disinherited by his brother. Regularly on Sundays he and I would walk across the Metal Bridge and out along the railway line and the low-lying fields to his birthplace. Fuming and scowling, he would twirl his stick and complain about weedy pastures or broken fences. I longed to call to the house to visit the outcast uncle whom I remembered vaguely as a big, soft-hearted, soft-spoken man but my father had other views and sternly forbade me ever to set foot on the place. We had great respect for his authority and would not easily go against his wishes, so we never did.

On his mother's side his roots were deep in Louth. His father had come from Armagh to marry into his mother's farm. And yet perversely he pulled his family from their roots many times. Dundalk, Carlow, Kilkenny, Ennis, back to Dundalk and finally to Limerick, where he died. But it was in Louth that my sixteen years of growing were spent and I suppose he and it have left a mark.

My sister and I once overheard our aunts referring to my father as 'that man' in the weary tones of women who have known too well the whims and vagaries of the other sex and had wished their sister to have been spared them. I thought it a wonderfully exciting thing that anyone should talk about my father at all and to refer to him as 'that man' was to make him interesting and mysterious, as unfathomable as his humours and moods. Indeed, it was one of his whims which uprooted us from Clare and brought us back to his native heath. He had built a new house in Ennis but objected to the shape of the porch and had a row with the builder whom he then decided to sue. In spite of pleas from my mother, his friends and all who had his interests at heart, he went ahead with the lawsuit and, of course, lost. He shook the dust of Clare off his heels and changed the course of our lives.

Unlike him, we were not natives, apart from my eldest sister who could boast a genuine pedigree because she had actually been born in Dundalk. The rest of us were Runners, and we would never quite shake off the taint of the West. I soon discovered that I was fair game for every gang fight and juvenile brawl in the district. I learned to run fast or fight hard. My accent provoked hilarity, my good manners contempt. 'Country gawk, come to Dundalk, to learn to use your knife and fork' and 'Maeve Kelly, broke her belly, sliding down a lump of jelly' were my introduction to the local lyric poetry. But I learned. I never quite learned how not to be the fall guy, but I did learn not to say, in response to What colour is your hair? 'I have fa-ir ha-ir,' splitting the syllables so that my new friends doubled up in mirth, or 'I went up the sta-irs.'

Gormless as any bumpkin at five, by the time I was nine I had ousted our gang leader by practising my jumps over the shucks all through the summer and then challenging her in the middle of winter to leap the deepest, widest ravine in the neighbourhood. When she drew back, her second in command leaped to save her honour and landed up to her neck in freezing December water. I can still recall the screams of her sister that their mother would kill her and I can remember thinking also that it was a poor mother who would not offer cocoa and bread and butter to her half-drowned child. There was a certain superiority to be gained from knowing one had a mother who would wrap one in a towel and say, 'Mhuishe, mhuishe, what were you doing at all,' in a soft Galway accent, without needing to hear the answer.

In spite of these minor disadvantages I grew to love that strange town even if I never got the West out of my blood. I came to terms with its humour and sardonic asides. I certainly learned to curb enthusiastic responses, which were always frowned on. Little by little, some of its iron entered my soul and to this day refuses to be dislodged.

I changed allegiance from one landscape to another, swapping the Hills of Clare for the Cooley Hills. I substituted the Metal Bridge and the train to Bellurgan and Gyles Quay

121 Pigeon Club, Drogheda, Co. Louth

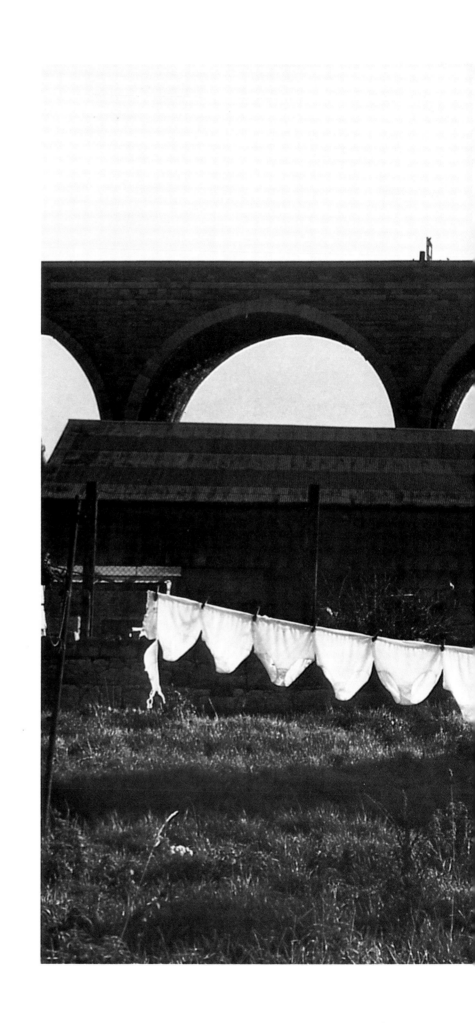

122 The lines, Drogheda, Co. Louth

for the West Clare Railway and the trips to Lahinch. I replaced in my memory the calmer, icy water of the east coast for the crashing, terrifying breakers of the West. I went with the rest of the family, all seven of us, on bicycle picnics to Blackrock where the tide went out so far it seemed to have forgotten to come back and we would rage if we had missed it and blame each other for delaying too long at home. I discovered the lovely countryside around the town. I picnicked with friends at the Long Woman's Grave and gloried in the views over Carlingford Lough. And I discovered the uncertainties of history and the politics of division.

When I was seventeen, on one of the hottest days of the summer, I mitched from school and cycled across the border to Newry where I was elbowed off the pavement by a 'B' Special because I asked him the time and he knew by my accent I was a papist bitch and I should go back where I belonged. A difficult thing for me to decide.

Each year, on the 'glorious twalfth', the town filled with immigrants from the North, who were occasionally denounced and preached at from the pulpit because they had littered the streets with their drunkenness. On one such twelfth as I was making one of my solitary forays into the countryside, a pony and trap carrying a couple waving their bottles of beer and singing nationalist songs at the tops of their voices passed me by at a canter. Something startled the pony and it bolted hell for leather along the road, eventually turning its occupants into the spiny blackthorn and whitethorn hedges. I watched the drama of rescue and the Redemptorist father in his long black robes reciting his prayers for the dying and then I ran home, away from the groans of the woman whose black hair had tumbled out from under her hat and whose blood had stained the road. Why had she run away from the Orange drums I wanted to know, only to lie by a ditch south of the border, her hair matted with gore, crying for mercy and forgiveness? No one could tell me. Only my father began a long detailed preamble which fossilised with its first sentence, 'You must remember that before all this.' Before all this? Before all this, I wanted to shout, there was nothing. Before all this there was no me.

And once I committed the grave sin of being in the company of others who shouted at our Protestant neighbour, 'Proddy, proddy, quack quack quack, run to the divil and never come back.' He called to our house to tell my father that I was not keeping good company and that he was disappointed and sad to see me join in their bigotry. My father looked at me with great dismay and, though he believed me when I told him I didn't join in, he said, 'Remember, birds of a feather fly together. You are judged by the company you keep.'

We finally settled in Mill Street, a higgledy-piggledy place with houses of many shapes and sizes and a view from upstairs across the quays to Anaverna. On its bog my father made unsuccessful attempts to save turf during the war. I had visions of lorry-loads of delicious-smelling black sods being deposited in our back garden to keep us warm for the remaining years of the war. But the turf stayed where it belonged and with it his good spade which he mourned afresh every time the mountain was mentioned. To this day I imagine it up there, embalmed no doubt for posterity, a curious memorial to his strange enthusiasms. I don't know why we never got the turf off the mountain any more than we never used the haybox in which we were supposed to be able to casserole either our food or our feet, perhaps both at the same time. In the 1940s there were many queer plans for making life more tolerable, like trying to turn parsnips into bananas, or roasting hawthorn leaves to add to the precious tea-leaves, or converting dandelion roots to the bitterest coffee imaginable. And there were war rumours and talk of battles lost and won. Once a plane dropped a bomb on the quay, shattering windows for miles around. We went to view the crater it left but we were not particularly impressed. There had been no casualties and some cynics began to doubt that it had been a bomb at all. Although we were relieved not to be bombed out like the English we were slightly ashamed that we hadn't any scars to show for the war. Being naturally interested in death and the business of dying and being also natural cowards, we would have liked the thrill of involvement without actually getting hurt ourselves.

But we had other death dramas to prepare us for adulthood. Before the war was over and before Noël Browne's Sanatoria had sprung up around the country, many of our friends and relations had died of tuberculosis. We lived next door to an undertaker. In the yard near the end of our back garden the coffins were shaped and planed. The black horses were stabled there. I often leaned across the wall to watch them being groomed for their majestic task and I thought of all the people, young and old, who would be pulled in the glass hearse to their last resting-place.

I grew up always aware of death. It was around us everywhere and it was part of our religious education. There were powerful sermons at the Redemptorist church, where graphic descriptions of souls in torment made the marrow in our bones satisfyingly chill. We didn't need any horror films. All we had to do to curdle our blood was attend a special course of sermons or a retreat for sinners. The latter was something of a problem for me since I had an obstinate belief in my own goodness and I could never believe myself to be a sinner. I often practised standing at the back of the church saying 'Lord be merciful to me a sinner,' but I had a sneaking sympathy for the Pharisee who said 'Thank God I am not like other men.' It was hard to be humble. But the thunderous orators tried their best. I could never quite reconcile the amiable, humorous men who joked and laughed with us as children with the frowning preachers whose voices rang with passion as they bewailed the wickedness of the world and the evils lurking in sinful hearts. But it was a joy to go to Confession to our favourite priest and to have a sweet pushed through the little space under the grille and to be told that we were very good and we need only say three Hail Marys, not for a penance because we were too good to need one, but for his very own intentions.

Between life and death, between good and evil, we were poised. Material possessions didn't bother us because all of our friends were in the same leaking boat of poverty. There was little advertising and little to buy in the shops. Our clothes were let down and passed from sister to sister or brother to brother. There was a dressmaker in the town who specialised in turning coats. She would carefully unrip the seams and restitch the whole garment. My mother had always loved Foxford tweeds and had coats made up for my sisters before our times grew hard. They saw us all through several winters until elbows poked through and patches were made from the pockets. I had a patch on my right elbow so I regularly went to school on the right-hand side of the road with the patch to the wall and returned on the other side for the same reason, until I

126 Drogheda Town, Co. Louth

rebelled and refused to wear the thing anymore. We had our own pride and our own sensitive areas and they were usually respected by our parents. My father was amused by our little rebellions although he roared if he thought they were getting out of hand. I don't know about my sisters and brothers, but I certainly knew when it was dangerous to give him cheek or answer him back. Perhaps I gave him more cheek because I had assessed the risk fairly accurately.

None the less, we all defied his poor attempts at showing off, like wanting to parade us up to the top of the church for Midnight Mass, the way the local bank manager did. He ushered his small flock to their seats and then stood in the aisle, stiff-necked and proud while they took their places. He used to look around just once, as if to say 'There you are now, see what I've done.' Then he would remove a large white hanky from his pocket, and shake it out with a flourish before placing it with the panache of a magician on the kneeling-board. One Christmas my father planned to do likewise and we knew better than to rebel openly. But each of us, as we entered the porch, made appropriate plans to foil him and save our own honour. One went to serve Mass, one to sing in the choir and the three uninitiated females to slip into seats behind him. That left only my mother to usher into the seat. His look of stupefaction when he turned around to find his flock of sheep had turned into wolves and had slunk away was worth anything. For the first quarter of an hour of the ceremony he kept turning around to glare at us. One of my sisters buried her face in her hands and made horrible groans of embarrassment. I always found my father's face a wondrously comical thing and the more he scowled the more I grinned until, in the end, he began to laugh too. It's a cherished memory of him, his ability to see the humour of the situation, even the misery of his own dying.

Our affection for him was well watered by our criticism of his very obvious and very human little failings. I think we all inherited from him a rather too judgemental and too critical attitude to humanity. From him we inherited sceptical and analytical minds which have not always served us well. He was proud of us and we knew it. He was proud of our good grades at school, but would now and again admonish us for being too clever. A little learning is a dangerous thing, he would quote, drink deep or taste not the Pierian Spring. He was a great talker and a great reciter. He could make his neighbours cry with the power and pathos of his recitation of 'The Green Eye of the Little Yellow God'. He had a marvellous long poem about the death of King Conor MacNessa and another about a priest's leap across a mighty chasm as he eludes pursuers. It was great rousing stuff, probably embarrassing to my sisters, but I was too naïve to know any better and I loved every syllable.

We never knew what tragedies he had in his own life because he never spoke of them. But there were photographs taken at the turn of the century of his three sisters and two of his brothers who were all dead before they were thirty. He would simply mention their names and sigh and say no more. He was healthily sceptical of politics and religion but managed to hold onto his faith and his pride in his country. He always said he was a Home Ruler although his brothers had been for complete separation. Somewhere in my mother's house is a newspaper cutting with a photograph of his brother Tommy hoisting the Nationalist flag over the monument in the town square, while the troops stood around for the proclamation of the accession of George V. My father would have distanced himself from such displays, but he acknowledged his brother's nerve in challenging the established order.

For me, Louth and my father go together. I never think of one without thinking of the other. I have not been back to Dundalk since the last trip we made when he knew that he had not much longer to live and he wanted to see his town again and to be reconciled with his brother who was also dying. They sat and talked with tears in their eyes in the parlour of the farmhouse on the land that had divided them for too much of their lives. That was in 1960. He died in March the following year. I sat and held his hand and he said, 'Never be too ambitious for your children. I have had too many ambitions but I have had good children and they have loved me.'

130 Pecker Dunne, taken near Duffy's Cross, Co. Louth

132 Into Connemara, Co. Galway

COUNTY GALWAY

Desmond Hogan

I'd seen her get on a train in Galway city February of the previous year. A chiffon scarf wrapped around her plentiful white hair. A stout woman carrying a small bag. On the way to Dublin she piped a myserious song: 'If you sit on a red hot poker it's the sign of an early spring.'

'Your memory must have gone with your looks,' she told a small, bespectacled man, standing over him, after having challenged him about some historical data. We never spoke but on the train from Holyhead, which had been greatly delayed, she sat near me, having been befriended by some Dublin boys who were emigrating. One of them had a penchant for 1950s songs and delivered *My Wild Irish Rose*, out in the aisle, a fashionable white polo neck on him, troubadour's thick quiff of blond hair on his forehead, in tribute to her. She and the boys left the train together at Euston. They were going to have bacon and eggs in a *caff* and then she was going to bring them to a nun in Wimbledon. She was on the deck of the boat that morning as it neared Dun Laoghaire, but as I got a lift to Galway that was the last I saw of her. First part of our town is Our Lady of Lourdes church in Creagh, standing up, alone there, like a tombstone. That is on the Roscommon side of the town. Then you cross a bridge and are in Galway. The mental hospital, which they started building in 1833, is on the Roscommon side of the town, but that doesn't save Galway from having the highest mental illness rate in Europe.

The smaller river which runs into the Suck had run dry – water-mint growing all over its basin, I found when I inspected it later on. This is where I used to meet my friends as a child. By the rivulet. A sanctuary. On the other side of it a carriageway, which circumvents the town, runs parallel to it now. The church nearby had to be built in a marsh by decree of the local landlord but its steeple rose in spite higher than the spires of the Protestant church which sits on a hill. Cardinal Wiseman was borne on the shoulders of local people for its consecration and Napoleon III sent a vestment with the Bonaparte badge on it for the occasion. These were the stories we grew up with, stories that have stayed alongside stories of local people: the Czech women who ran a jewellery shop in town once. They had shunted and shifted all over Ireland, finding peace here for a while, then retired, lived in a house in Clontarf Dublin, the eldest leaving me a table-cloth in her will, the youngest having died recently in an old people's home on the other side of Galway city among the rocks, the anarchic cabbage seed.

I'd visited Prague since last I'd been in the town. In the old Jewish cemetery there I'd thought of them and in the suburbs of Prague, under high-rise flats, a gipsy family on a bench waiting for a bus, I'd thought of the gipsies, the tinkers who'd encircled our town in winter when I was a child. They'd created a pattern for the lives of many of my contemporaries, a pattern of moving on, always moving on, nomads.

'Ah, Dagenham,' a woman had said in a buffet in Prague, 'Dagenham,' pulling at a hair on my naked arm. She'd been there once. I lived not far from Dagenham, near by a settlement of Irish travellers. I sometimes went there and heard stories about County Galway. How families of tinkers were turned away from cinemas there and spent the

136 Mountainside, Co. Galway

night instead reading comics by rural camp-fires. How tinkers got married there with rings made from teaspoons. Matchstick barrel-caravans were produced, possibly as memorials to County Galway. My town was quietly referred to, renowned and sacred because of its annual horse fair. In Gill's Hotel in Ballinasloe the local dignitaries gathered each year during the fair to celebrate the town, its achievements in the previous year. Now the town has meandered way outside its former tight nucleus, lizards of new streets, new avenues, a new type of child on their pavements, the streets, the avenues cutting into Garbally estate. The heir to the manor, much to the chagrin of his father, had once married a Cockney music hall artiste, Isabel Bilton. She was loved by all when she became lady of the manor and her legend lingered right up to my childhood in the 1950s. I think I was very lucky. Galway imploded with stories, many of them too intense ever to write down. Perhaps the best stories we carry with us, within us, never to be written down. But there was always a sense of making something from experience. In Naughton's pub in Galway city as I entered, a young man on a bar stool belted out a song he might have made up himself.

'There's not enough work in this country,
There's not enough land to go round.'

Galway Arts Festival was on, at night the streets around the Claddagh jammed with young people drinking beer, wine, the odd guitarist among them, crouched on the ground, drawing his audience. On the walls by the canal the sexuality of Jesuit boys was impugned, the IRA praised. A giant puppet of Gulliver, which had recently taken part in the Dublin millennium parade, was outstretched on a beach near Salthill. By Claddagh Bridge were a newly sown wild cherry tree and Italian maple-tree. They might have been sown, in this city of youth, for some of County Galway's defeated and exiled, the Czech lady who'd ended her days west of Galway city when in fact her home had been east of it.

For years when I got to Galway Clifden, in the north-west of it, was the first place I headed to. Another garrison town like Ballinasloe to the very east of it. But this time I'd dallied in the town I was from, in Galway city. I've stayed with the same old lady for years in Clifden. She's become my great friend. In her mid-seventies, much of the time on buses in Ireland, on her way to see Oliver Plunkett's head in Drogheda, making a pilgrimage to Lough Derg. You'll often see her between buses, at a bus stop, in a tracksuit. In Drogheda once at the opening of a disco the DJ asked her if he could put blue in her hair and dance with her. She was after a day's praying so why not? But the blue didn't come out for six months. One of her many stories. Like the story of how, in her négligé, she was attacked by a fox and her only fear was that her dead body would be found naked. A picture of Our Lady of Medugorje, the latest Lady, over the mantelpiece. 'I could have filled the field with all the boy-friends I had.' The stories continued into the night. She was married twice but both her husbands are long dead. Her children live in Galway city. One of her sons, his wife and two adopted children went to London the previous Christmas, intending to stay, but returned after a brief sojourn to poverty in Galway. 'The moment we cease to hold each other, the moment we break faith with one another, the sea engulfs us and the light goes out,' James Baldwin wrote somewhere. There may be few jobs in Galway city but there is an enfolding, a mantling sense of community.

138 Towards the ocean, Co. Galway

In Galway city I'd seen a former heroin-addict friend dance in an old church converted into an arts centre. It might have been a dance from a Yeats play. *The Herne's Egg*, for instance. He was alone there in the centre of the floor.

> The real world, the otherworld, is behind us and beyond us, out of our ken, and all we are aware of is the vague shadow of reality flickering in the things we see.

One of the last lines of the Ballinasloe poet Eoghan O Tuairisc came back to me as I watched the boy dance, for he too was from Ballinasloe, Eoghan O Tuairisc having been a shoemaker's son who saw a notice pinned on a tree one day that he'd got first place in a scholarship examination for Garbally Boys' School, then was told he couldn't take up the scholarship for unstated reasons, only being allowed in through the backhand intercession of powerful people in the town, a renowned headmaster at Saint Grellan's National School for instance. He went on to a life of poetry, switching betwen Gaelic and English, part of the immaculate, the healing heritage of this boy who danced in the arts centre.

Clifden was ragged on a summer night. Harp music coming from a hotel, a ballad being bawled out from a pub opposite the hotel. A few old ladies, scarves on them, walking the streets, picking up bits of gossip from one another. There's no shortage of gossip in Clifden in summer and even in winter sometimes there's excitement — like the winter when an American woman bought the old gaol-house, intending to open it as a hotel for American ghosts. But the plan never worked out and the ghosts stayed on the other side of the Atlantic.

Beyond Clifden, north of it and still in County Galway, is Cleggan. About fifteen years ago I went to a wake in the Pier Bar, the ninety-year-old proprietress laid out, and I said to her sprightly daughter, 'Sorry about the death of your sister.' Tall candles burned about the corpse. Another time in the same pub I saw two small, squat men dance a jig together to celebrate May Day. Seven miles out to sea from Cleggan is Inishbofin. Theodore Roethke lived there for a while, one of the most westerly parts of Galway, but was carted back after a few months, drunk out of his head, in a strait-jacket, to the most easterly point of Galway – Ballinasloe Mental Hospital. The conundrum being that Ballinasloe Mental Hospital is actually in Roscommon. Despite this catastrophic vignette there's a serene lyric by Roethke on a plaque in a pub on Bofin:

> I suffered for birds, for young rabbits caught in the mower,
> My grief was not excessive
> For to come upon warblers in early May
> Was to forget time and death.

About six o'clock in the morning, my third day in Clifden, the phone rang. My friend's brother-in-law had just died in County Roscommon. There were phone calls made to relatives all over the world. The subject changed. 'The wedding was out of this world.' And by seven one of her sons had arrived in his car and shortly we were racing through the Connemara morning. There are many stories that this county had given me, stories that tumbled out at the worst of times; the story of a ninety-year-old tinker woman who insisted on being brought from Portiuncula Hospital, Ballinasloe, to the side of the road in Aughrim because she said she wanted to die in the open air, and then rose and lived to see Croydon again; my friend the guard in Galway city who on his retirement, only having been out of Ireland once before, working as a labourer on a building site in London in his teens, packed his things in his car, drove to Portugal, and purchased a hut on a beach there where he still lives.

'He brought in a good crop of turf the summer before he left,' the same man had recently commented to me in Portugal about the boy who'd left Ballinasloe when he was sixteen and had since prospered in London – as if his prosperity was a reward for his diligence with the turf. The former guard had been posted in Ballinasloe then. Would that such pleasing omens attended us all. But there is a sense of strength from such language, a trustfulness that mistakes, misfortune can be absolved and that we can start all over again.

'There was a man who lived in a remote part of County Galway and he wasn't very bright and he slept on a hard board. So he got very bad arthritis. The advice he got was to sleep on a feather bed. He put one feather on the floor and slept on it. His arthritis became much worse and he shouted out, "But what would it be like if I slept on a whole bed of feathers!"' My friend told a story as we raced to the house of the dead man, tinker encampments more profuse in north-east Galway – oilskins thrown over random armchairs – half-wrecked gateposts bearing shaven posters for showbands, pilgrimages to Lourdes, bingo, national schools more isolated and perished-looking, homesteads more beseeching, a congestion of car tyres in one field, and the stories kept coming, long after we'd crossed the border into Roscommon.

141 Bottom of Garraun Mountain, Co. Galway

142 Lake Fee, Co. Galway

144 Farmers at rest, Co. Fermanagh

COUNTY FERMANAGH

Frank Ormsby

Fermanagh is in the news again. Fermanagh is always in the news. On the front pages and on the back pages, in the small print and in the large, among the football results and the nature notes. In books about fishing and pot-holing, agriculture and industry, drainage schemes, folklore, ancient monuments. In tourist brochures and National Trust pamphlets, in local histories, in development reports and among statistics about the unemployed. Like every other place I know, it ripples perpetually outwards in the memory and imagination, renewing and recreating itself, familiar and elusive and forever strange.

So I read about the latest political squabble in the Council chambers, or the latest milk-churn bomb exploding in a culvert on a country road, or the inconvenience caused to the remoter farming communities by the authorities' decision to crater an unapproved border road, and the news is old news. Until I learn that the rare orchid *spiranthes romanzoffiana* has turned up in a garden in Enniskillen, or that someone has spotted *quercusia quercus*, the Purple Hairstreak butterfly, in Pobble Forest, or that a large bat, previously thought to be extinct, has come to light in the caves of Boho. And I'm willingly chastened again into seeing how presumptuous is the claim to 'know' any place.

For me the ripples started in the townland of Makeny, about a mile and a half from the village of Irvinestown, on the main Enniskillen road. We lived in what amounted to a valley. The road wound out of sight a few hundred yards away on either side. The three houses immediately visible from ours were on a higher level and formed a rough circle around us; and we did not own a car, so that family outings were unusual, if they took place at all. Lough Erne played no part in my early childhood. It was miles away and inaccessible. I was eleven before I saw Devenish Island, for example, and even then it was only the top of the round tower glimpsed daily from a bus window as I travelled to and from college in Enniskillen. Meanwhile, the world in the vicinity of the house was manageable and its variety infinite, a world in which every field and landmark had its name – not 'Fermanagh' as yet, but the Brown Ground, the Brick Hole, Donnelly's Bog, the Long Bottom, the Green Lane, the Two Trees.

Directly opposite the zinc bungalow where we lived were the woods we called the Plantation, and a short distance away the mottled railings and dilapidated gate-lodge at the main entrance to the Castle Irvine or Necarne Castle Estate. Playing in those woods, or even venturing into the empty castle through an open window, had the appeal of the illicit. The castle grounds were, in fact, open to the public but it was more of an adventure to lie under the rhododendrons like trespassers as Captain Richard Herman's car glided over the pot-holes, or to duck behind the big chestnut tree at the sound of the gamekeeper's jeep.

The castle itself was history. It reached back to the days of the Lowther family, who had founded Lowtherstown, and the Irvines, who had changed the name to Irvinestown, its greystone battlements and coat of arms conferring an antiquity that was somehow both remote and satisfying. The remains of an American and British hospital camp from the Second World War were history too, but we never thought of them in that way. The circular, earth-covered burrows of the air raid shelters with their damp, vegetable darkness and dull echoes, the stone floors like a series of intersecting pavements where the Nissen huts had stood, the earthwork that might have been a trench or the site of a gun emplacement, the piles of rusted beer cans in corners of the undergrowth – these were special attractions of the natural playground that surrounded our house.

The estate had its characteristic sounds – the dangerous modulations of a chain-saw and the crashing of trees, the frantic gear-wrenching and gravel-rending of rally drivers time-trialling among red and white bollards, the yowling of hounds, the blattering and keening of beaters during the annual shoot, the panic-stricken explosion of pheasants across the main road. Most familiar of all was the sound of gunfire – the shotguns of the hunters, the gamekeeper, the clay pigeon shooters, and often, in the long evenings, the rifle-fire of the 'B' Specials practising in the castle grounds. There were characteristic sights and smells too – the grisly tree on which hung the rotting bodies of grey crows, magpies and other scavengers, the suppurating rabbits, blind and swollen with myxomatosis, which crawled onto the avenue to die.

When we began to think of Fermanagh as an entity, one piece of the thirty-two-part jigsaw that was the map of Ireland, it seemed a peculiarly isolated place, one of those limbo-like, half-lost border counties, like Monaghan and Cavan, roughly equidistant from the centres of power. There were villages like Belleek, Pettigo and Belcoo, that seemed to straddle the border, and houses in the border sector which seemed to belong to neither Northern Ireland nor the Republic. To travel from one end of the county to the other was to hear people's accents take on a Donegal or Cavan or Monaghan twang. Yet, in spite of these shades and gradations, the political boundary was there, denied by the landscape and the dialects on either side of it, but visible as customs posts, road-blocks, the place-names in both English and Irish on the signposts in the Republic, and as palpable in our minds and imaginations as if it had been a broad white band painted across roads and farms. It was palpable too in the tension and division that permeated almost every aspect of life in Fermanagh. Among the lakes, drumlins and housing estates of that deceptively placid, postcard county, a defensive Unionist minority, who controlled local government, and a Catholic majority, resentful of discrimination against them in housing and employment, squared up to each other perennially, loathed each other's festivals and sometimes shed blood.

When I went to St Michael's College in Enniskillen in 1959, we were packed into St Michael's Reading Rooms, a parochial recreation centre attached to the school buildings in Belmore Street. Next door was the dark green hush of the snooker room. Outside the window the River Erne flowed under the East Bridge and the people of Enniskillen walked past above on the Queen Elizabeth Road. All around was a townscape that told a convoluted story. From the Forthill, General Galbraith Lowry-Cole, a hero of the Peninsular War, looked over the houses from his fluted Doric column. At one end of Belmore Street, in Gaol Square, was the obelisk commemorating the Inniskilling Regiment in the South African War and at the other, under the gable of the Reading Rooms, the Great War Memorial, a bronze soldier on a granite plinth with his head

147 Christian recital, Enniskillen, Co. Fermanagh

bowed in prayer. Here the ripples seemed both local and global. Here, too, on Poppy Day 1987, the troubled history of a border county converged more devastatingly than usual, a variant of the history that had converged earlier on Ballykelly, Darkley and other places.

So Fermanagh is in the news again. Fermanagh is always in the news. I hear that the County Council has a scheme to plant willow forests for the production of methane. I read about the restoration of Castle Coole's Palladian grandeur, about the coming attractions at the Ardhowen Arts Centre, about Enniskillen Flying Club and Enniskillen Agricultural College, and about trampolining at the Lakeland Forum. I follow Lisnaskea Emmets and Lisnarick Rangers, Teemore Shamrocks and Irvinestown Wanderers up and down the league tables. I learn that the Remembrance Day bombing has given impetus to a new programme for mutual understanding in schools – and note, without surprise, that the programme has already been condemned as a plot to 'teach Protestant and Unionist children the tenets of Romanism and the political system of Irish Republicanism'.

Some day soon I'll make a trip to William Blake's pub in Enniskillen and the Clock Bar in Derrygonnelly, visit White Island and Davy's Island and Belleek Pottery, mingle with the continental fishermen, the tourists cruising the lough, the canoeists and water-skiers at Carry Bridge. I'll climb Topped Mountain for the first time, perhaps, and make my first descent into the Marble Arch caves.

And the ripples that have never stopped spreading will begin again – accumulating, accommodating, reflecting from a hundred angles that indefinable, irreducible, unforgettable place.

149 Farmers at work, Co. Fermanagh

150 A cup of tea, Co. Fermanagh

COUNTY TIPPERARY

Nuala Ní Dhomhnaill

'How are your veins?'

I barely smother a facetious reply: 'Very well, thank you, and yours?' This is deadly serious. In both my parents' medical opinion I am severely overweight and liable to die on the spot any minute from cardiac arrest. So at 8.00 a.m. on a dark December morning my father is trying to get 10cc of blood out of me for cholesterol and other tests. He can't find a vein. 'You might as well be trying to get blood from a turnip,' I hear him mutter as the third one collapses. As he withdraws the syringe in disgust a sudden gush of blood spurts out. I faint. 'Quare class of doctor you'd have made.' I smile in secret self-justification. I always said...

Later that morning we head off for the Silvermine Mountains and Templederry, in Irish Sléibhte an Airgid, 'the Mountains of Silver', and Teampall Doire, 'the Church of the Oak Grove'. It is a long time since either silver or oak groves were found in these parts, yet it still remains a place all of its own. My father can't get out on the road soon enough. What with the days that are in it, light is scarce. Soon we are in Tipperary, on the road to Nenagh, which I first travelled one day at the end of August 1958, snatched from my idyllic fosterage with my Aunt May in the Kerry Gaeltacht. Nobody had much of an idea where we were going. Earlier in England, when my father had announced that he was applying for the job of County Surgeon there, he was greeted with some incredulity. Nenagh, for Christ's sake, where on earth was that? My mother who had done her geography through Irish could not be persuaded that it was even in Munster. Perfectly ensconced in her own private practice in Lancashire, it sounded to her like the back of beyond. Somewhere in the dreaded midlands. The Doldrums of Ireland. The Horse Latitudes. Nevertheless, being a good Irish Catholic, she gave in and followed her husband. And so, that autumn of 1958, a mountainy tribe, we descended on the huge three-storey house which until then had belonged to three Protestant spinster sisters. Baptists they were, 'Dippers' in the local parlance. Not that I knew much of the local parlance then, or even later. For one thing, we spoke Irish at home, and this was the black 'Galltacht', a bastion of colonists since the Middle Ages. We were blow-ins, ever to remain so. And after fifteen years we blew out very much as we had blown in.

The house was dark, north-facing, most of the rooms having been painted in bottle green, for no explicable reason. But it boasted what had once been a meticulously kept garden. Abandoned over the summer while the house lay empty, it was now stupendously and promiscuously overgrown. At age six you could get as easily lost in the herbaceous border as in any upstairs room where the monumental furniture had the uncanny habit of falling on you. Stalking through the elephant grass, we fell upon Damask roses with no less avidity than hunters in India on tigers. Years later in seed catalogues I was gradually to learn the names of some of the flowers – lupins, columbines, delphiniums, cosmos, aquilegia – but at that time we stared at them like beings from another planet. They were deliciously dangerous and exotic. And poisonous of course. After all, one of them wasn't called 'anemone' (an enemy) for nothing. If you ate one you would surely die. The only 'good' flowers were the peony roses and this because they were in great demand for petal-strewing on Corpus Christi. And there were also trees. Never in my short personal history – spent until then in a mining town in Lancashire or the wind-swept seaboard of West Kerry – never had I seen the likes of the trees of the rich farmlands of North Tipperary. Huge trees. Good climbable trees. Trees you would never ever want to come down from.

But it was not all trees and peonies. Most of the time you had to go to school, to nuns. Sister Agnes, in first class, who sewed ignominious lengths of brown paper on the dress of any unfortunate seven-year-old whose skirts were high enough to expose the kneecaps. Miss Maguire, in second class, a lay teacher at least, but constantly chewing lozenges and giving you slobbery wet kisses. Sister Paul who boxed your ears. Sister Pius who got you reading by the then innovatory pedagogical brainwave of starting a class library. Sister Peter, in sixth class, who had an old, flat, well-seasoned stick that stung like hell. All I remember of the school building itself is an upstairs glass case, dating back to when biology was still part of the primary school course, which had rows of spiders, butterflies and bumble-bees laid out neatly for inspection. On the rarely-used front stairs was an oil painting of Patrick Sarsfield at the Siege of Limerick. Cannon-balls hurtled over walls that the French General, St Ruth, said could be knocked down with roasted apples. When my mother asked the principal, Sr Lawrencia, why there was no scholarship class to prepare for the County Council scholarship exam, she was informed that there was no demand for one: 'Most of the girls around here will work behind the counter in shops for a few years before settling down and getting married.' All of which increased my mother's disdain for these denizens of the fat lands, the cream of Ireland, *mar dhea*, rich and thick; '*Ina luí go spadánta ar na bánta*', 'Lying around lethargically in the grasslands', like the bovine specimens they were. Penning an excuse of rheumatic fever, she used to take me out of school for three weeks at a time and teach me herself.

The fact that we spoke Irish at home didn't exactly help either. When any school pals I might have had came around to our house my father met them at the door, spouting Irish at them. They ran off and that was often the last I saw of them. Know your friends, indeed. Then my granny came to live with us. She was of the spare-the-rod-and-spoil-the-child persuasion and I soon found out that in any dispute that might arise between us, I invariably came off second-best, as, no matter what evidence to the contrary, my mother always took her side. She also hated my father and so we children immediately rallied to his defence. I learned to keep my big mouth shut and my nose stuck in a book instead. Because the marriage ban was still in operation, my mother could get no job as a doctor. At one stage she volunteered to help the diocesan pilgrimage to Lourdes in her medical capacity. When she went down to the garda station to get a passport, she discovered that she had to get her husband's permission to leave the country. To an independently-minded woman in her late thirties, who had previously run a large practice on her own, going always in good Gaeltacht fashion under her maiden name, this was the last straw. The tension mounted.

153 Turnstiles, Co. Tipperary

154 Stalls, Co. Tipperary

On Sundays we used to go to eleven o'clock Mass. To avoid the inevitable traffic jam afterwards, we often took a back road home, around by the ruins of the old Franciscan Priory. There, at a place called Sherlock's Field, was a large sign proclaiming to my barely-lettered eye: 'Trespassers will be Persecuted' ... Now I knew all about persecution – wasn't that the Christians being thrown to the lions? And you mean to tell me that just for stepping on that land, putting your big toe in, maybe, that you would be punished by being thrown to lions? It did seem awfully strict. But then such was the emotional minefield that we tiptoed through at the time that nothing seemed impossible. And after all, wasn't this the very selfsame field that a man was working in on a Sunday with his *seisreach* ('plough team') and plough when the first bell went for Mass in the Priory behind him? Then the second bell went and the third and still he paid no heed. Then what do you know but didn't the ground open up and swallow him, horses and plough and all. *'Obair Dhomhnaigh, ni maith i,'* 'Sunday work is not a good thing,' as my granny would pronounce from the corner, nodding more violently than ever to make up for the understatement of the proverb. About this time my father bought a half-breed pointer bitch named Belle, short for Jezebel, or so I was told. 'What kind of name is that then, Jezebel?' 'A biblical name.' 'But who was it?' 'Go and read your Bible and find out.' Being the kind of obnoxious child I was, I went and did just that. But I was still pretty confused. It all seemed very mysterious. Apparently, there was this queen who got into awful trouble and ended up dead with her guts being eaten by dogs. And all for nothing, it seemed, except for painting her face, in other words wearing make-up. You mean to tell me just for wearing make-up ... Awfully strict it all seemed. Terrible strict.

The only place we really felt at home was up in the mountains. The Silvermines, up Step and Glen Coloo, by the side of Keeper Hill or beyond in Templederry where my father leased the shooting rights on half of a hill named Cooneen, right across from a slightly higher one which rejoiced in the much more unlikely name of Bolingbroke. Here we trained gun dogs, burned heather in strips to encourage the young growth beloved of grouse, built quarefangled traps for scaldcrows. I still know every inch of those hills and if necessary could walk them barefoot and blindfold.

An elaborate code of reciprocity soon developed with the upland people. The odd goitre or hernia got patched up in return for cups of tea and bottles of a more potent brew innocently presented as 'holy water', which was the world's own power for flaming the Christmas pudding. Once even the garda superintendent himself asked my father if he knew where you could get good poteen hereabouts. Naturally, he never let on. Still, even in the mountains you were never unobserved. My mother was in the habit of bringing along the Sunday newspaper on these upland jaunts, and used to sit down on a ditch when the endless quartering back and forward after dogs was getting too much for her. One day a man accosted her. From his rig-out it was obvious that he was a countryman taking a short cut home over the hill after staying on a mite too long in the pub after Mass. He approached her warily. He was very inquisitive. The more he asked her what she considered personal questions, the more she spun him a tissue of lies, to put him off the scent. He bade her farewell most courteously, then turned tail and ran pell-mell down to Maddens', the nearest house. 'Quick, quick,' he shouted, 'send for the guards. There is a madwoman escaped from the mad-house in

Clonmell, didn't I hear it on the radio in the morning, and she's up there on the hill, I just met her.' It was with great difficulty that they managed to persuade him that the woman he saw on the hill wasn't stark raving mad. After all, what grown woman in her sound mind would travel half-way up a hill in order to find a ditch to read her paper on!

Recalling that incident, this evening by the warmth of the Stanley range with Katie, the last surviving Madden:

'And don't you remember, doctor, that you met that very same man in this house the Christmas after?'

'So I did, Katie. I remember it well. And we had a whale of a time blackguarding him.'

'Yes, you kept on drawing him out.'

'"I've heard tell of you," I said to him. "Aren't you the man who met the madwoman up on the hill?" "Yes," said he, "she was mad all right. I couldn't get a word of sense out of her. A quare wan she was entirely."'

Tears of laughter run down Katie's rosy girl-like cheeks.

'"Oh Willie, Willie," sez I, trying to warn him.'

'"And this madwoman, what did she look like?" I asked him. "Did she look like me now?" "Ah no, missus," he said, "she didn't look like you at all. That wan had fat thighs."'

At which my mother, *sotto voce* to me in Irish, *'Bíonn an fhírinne searbh,'* 'Truth is bitter.'

Earlier I had sent the children back to the house. The adults, who had gone off with guns, were still nowhere in sight. I followed my nose to a spot I remembered from my childhood, Raven's Rock, where a large outcrop of shale hangs over a bend in the river. I scrambled over rough ground until I was within a magic circle of sound caused by the rapids before and beyond the bend. I still felt weak from the fainting fit of the morning. Suddenly I knew what I must do. I took off my boots and socks and rolled up my pants as high as they would go, and waded into the river. It wasn't easy. There were sharp pebbles underfoot. It was bitterly cold but I knew that if I could ford the river and touch the rock I would be grounded at last, safe from the vague memories and half-forgotten fears of my childhood that had been following me about all day like so many bad dreams. Against walking vampires and bloodletters, father figures who go about with guns, quarrelsome grannies and nuns with big sticks, fields you would be thrown to lions for sticking your big toe in, meadows that would suddenly open and swallow you up, dogs that would eat you just for wearing make-up, walls that could be knocked down by roasted apples, Spanish wine that brings no hope, the help that never came from the Pope, rock and water of Templederry, deliver us.

Carraig na Bhfiach

'Tá ceithre creasa ar an ndomhan,
leanaigh do cheann is geobhair eolas'
a dúirt an tseanbhean liom sa taibhreamh,
i siúd a chasann an domhan mór ar a fhearsaid,

is maidin gheimhridh leanaim na comharthaí sóirt
a aithním sa ghrian, sa talamh is san aer
is téim i ndiaidh mo shróine síos le sruth
na habhann chomh fada leis an gcor ag Carraig na bhFiach.

Trasna uaim tá faill dhorcha sceallachloch
ag gobadh amach chomh modhmharách le beann
is timpeall orm tá ciorcal draiochta glóir
ós na clocha corra im' dhiaidh is Poll an Easa romham.

Siúlaim isteach san abhainn. Tá sé garbh fuar.
Ba dhóigh leat mo dhá chois reoite ag an oighear,
ach leanaim i gcónai ag cur coise romham
go sroichim an bhruach eile thall, faoi sciathán den bhfaill.

Tá luibh Eoin Baiste dreoite istigh i scoilt
is ceannaíocha dubha ó anuraidh mar gheosadáin,
tá caonach chomh tiubh le duileascar na gcloch
ag fás ins an bhfothain is ribíní fada eidhneáin.

Tógaim mo cheann; tá an chuilinn fós go glas
is an bheith go niamhrach grástúil os mo chionn.
Croithim sceach gheal is titeann brat sceachóirí le sruth
is ithim ceann nó dhó acu in éagmais cnó

coille a shlogann an bradán is faigheann fios.
Mo ghrua i gcoinne na cloiche gheibhim deis
teacht chugham féin arís slán ón mbearna baoil,
mo cheann a chruinniú, bheith préamhaithe sa talamh is saor

ó arrachtaí na samhlaíochta is ós na deamhain aeir.

Raven's Rock

'There are four zones in the world/follow your head and you'll find a way'/the old woman said to me in a dream/she who turns the great globe on its axis

so now, a winter morning, I follow the signs/I read in the sun, the landscape and the sky/and following only my nose go down the stream/as far as the sudden bend at Raven's Rock.

Across from me the high dark cliff of shale/stands as majestically as a mountain peak/ and all about a magic circle of sound/from the rapids behind me and Poll an Easa before.

I step into the river. It is bitterly cold/You'd swear my legs were frozen solid in the icy stream/but I keep doggedly putting one leg before/the other till I reach the other bank, under an outcrop of the cliff.

A stem of St John's wort still standing in a cleft/last year's knapweed, so many withered stalks/moss grows as thick as any dyer's moss/and long ribbons of ivy trailing down the rocks.

I raise my head. The holly always green/and the naked birch shining and graceful growing above/I shake a hawthorn branch and a shower of haws/falls into the water. I eat one or two in lieu

of the hazel-nuts the salmon ate before and knew/all wisdom. My cheek resting against the rock I get a chance/to regain my composure, to skirt the gap of danger/ to gather my thoughts, grounded at last and free

of the monsters of the imagination, and the demons of the air.

160 Gambling, Co. Armagh

COUNTY ARMAGH

Paul Muldoon

Cauliflowers

Plants that glow in the dark have been developed through gene-splicing, in which light-producing bacteria from the mouths of fish are introduced to cabbage, carrots and potatoes.

The National Enquirer

More often than not he stops at the headrig to light
his pipe
and try to regain
his composure. The price of cauliflowers
has gone down
two weeks in a row on the Belfast market.

From here we can just make out
a platoon of Light
Infantry going down
the road to the accompaniment of a pipe-
band. The sun glints on their silver-
buttoned jerkins.

My uncle, Patrick Regan,
has been leaning against the mudguard
of the lorry. He levers
open the bonnet and tinkers with a light
wrench at the pipe-
line that's always going down.

Then he himself goes down
to bleed oil into a jerry-can.
My father slips the pipe
into his scorch-marked
breast pocket and again makes light
of the trepanned cauliflowers.

All this as I listened to lovers
repeatedly going down
on each other in the next room . . . 'light
of my life . . .' in a motel in Oregon.
All this. Magritte's
pipe

and the pipe-
bomb. White Annetts. Gillyflowers.
Margaret,
are you grieving? My father going down
the primrose path with Patrick Regan.
All gone out of the world of light.

All gone down
the original pipe. And the cauliflowers
in an unmarked pit, that were harvested by their own light.

163 In the mall, Co. Armagh

164 Carrick on Shannon, Co. Leitrim

COUNTY LEITRIM

John McGahern

Not many people live in Leitrim. The towns are small, the county town of Carrick-on-Shannon even smaller than the lesser towns of most other counties. Small here is mostly plain. A few have individual charm, but most of the towns are made up of one wide street, the houses in such tired argument with one another that they take on a drab sameness, and they are particularly weary in rain. Yet, people love these towns. That changes them on certain days and hours.

There is nothing dramatic about the landscape, but it is never dull. On the low drumlins around the countless lakes the soil is hardly an inch deep. Beneath it is the channel, compacted gravel, or daub, a sticky blue clay, and neither can soak up the heavy rainfall. Irregular hedgerows of whitethorn, ash, green oak, holly, wild cherry, sloe and sycamore divide the drumlins into rushy fields. The sally is the first to green and the first to wither; the rowan berries an incredible orange in the light from the lakes each September. The hedges are full of mice and insects and small birds, and sparrow-hawks can be seen hunting all through the day. The snipe and the otter, the pheasant and the grey-suited heron, the fox and the hare are common. Along the lake edges and river banks there are private lawns speckled with fishbones and blue crayfish shells where the otter feeds and trains her young. The foxglove is here and the orchid with thousands of other wild flowers.

Yet everywhere the ruined cottages in their little shelter of trees say what the goat said to the farmer when he insisted that the animal climb onto the roof to graze: 'The view up here is great, but there's nothing to eat, and even I am in danger of sliding off.'

An absurd couple of miles of coastline squeezes out to the Atlantic between Donegal and Sligo. From there Leitrim wanders shapelessly south and east to where the Shannon leaves the county at Roosky. The long stretch of Lough Allen splits the county in two. The low ridges of the Iron Mountains run for many miles from Lough Allen and cross the border as far as Florence Court. The upper Shannon flows out of Lough Allen past the tiny village that gives the county its name, passing through Carrick, Jamestown, Drumsna to Roosky. In the War of Independence and the Civil War there were men who fought the boredom and humiliation of gaols by walking together in their imagination up one side of a river bank in the morning, returning down the other side in the evening, each man picking out what the others had missed on the way. They knew the river stretches like their own lives.

Except for football and politics, the county divisions mean little to the people. For those who live on the Shannon, North Leitrim might as well be Cornwall. It is each single enclosed locality that matters and everything that happens within it is of passionate interest to those who live there. 'Do you have news — any news?' But once that news crosses a certain boundary eyes that a moment before were wild with curiosity will suddenly glaze. News no longer local is of no interest.

The dramas can be as funny or mundane or heartbreaking as the point of view. A man visits the garda station, complaining about the trespassing cattle of a close neighbour. 'The law wouldn't want to get involved. Why don't you have a word with him yourself? The two of you together could come to some agreement,' the Donegal guard advises reasonably. 'We're not speaking.' 'Why aren't you speaking?' 'We haven't spoken to one another in years.' 'What is the cause?' 'To tell you the truth I forget. It happened such a long time ago that I can no longer remember.' The situation is not dissimilar to what is taking place on a larger scale in Northern Ireland.

Their neighbours would not have forgotten. They know everything about one another. Each scrap of news is added gleefully to an enormous store. Both the individual and the family are held in high regard. They attend the same church, shop in the same shops in town, drink in the same bars: 'You go where your comrades go.' There is no getting away from the Drumshanbo wind.

A boy who had newly arrived in New York went looking for a cousin who had joined the police. He found him on duty on the East River. A piercing January wind blew off the water. As soon as they had shaken hands, he turned his back to the river saying, 'Michael, there's no escaping the wind from Drumshanbo.'

Our village is Fenagh: two bars watch one another across a road, one Fianna Fail, the other Fine Gael. The site of the one public telephone is a major focus. For the time being, anyhow, it stands outside the Fianna Fail bar, but a change of government could see it on the move again, all of thirty yards to the other side of the road. Overlooking the bars are two roofless fifteenth-century churches, all that remains of a once-great monastery founded by St Colmcille, internationally famous as a divinity school under St Killian, leaving us the *Book of Fenagh*. In the fields surrounding the monastery, paths between the rows of the monks' cells can be still traced in the short, rich grass. A purpose-built national school disfigures the ancient site.

A mile further on towards Mohill is the eyesore of a ruined ballroom that throbbed to the big bands of the 1950s. 'There wasn't a haycock safe for a mile around in the month of July.' All the money the ballroom made was lost on two other less securely-rooted ventures – a motor-cycle wall-of-death and an unheated swimming-pool dug by hundreds of workers amid all the lakes around. On the maps and signposts the lake below the house is Lough Rowan, but no one knows it other than as Laura Lake, 'the middle lake' in Gaelic, which is exactly what it is, a lake between two lakes.

Mohill is the town. In its plain way I think it beautiful. There is no desolate big street. The simple streets link perfectly into one another. A stark Catholic church on the hill dominates the town, the little Protestant church is hidden away in its graveyard garden at the bottom. Mohill is about as far south as the Ulster Plantation reached, and here Protestants can be found making a living on smallholdings as poor as those belonging to their Catholic neighbours. I like the town best in winter, the outskirts glistening with frost, the excitement on the faces of people in from the countryside for the late Saturday-night shopping, children and parcels being dragged about under the street-lamps. When the shopping is done, they go to the bars to meet the people they know and to discover the news, each locality to its own bar. Late winter, on a Thursday market-day, once I see the bags of seed potatoes and bundles of cabbage plants – Early

York and Flat Dutch, Greyhound and Curly – on the corner outside Luke Earley's, each bundle tied with baler twine of all colours, I know the winter is almost over. I think of it as one of the happiest towns in the world.

Outside the county I heard a barman ask a fairly old man with a thick Leitrim accent, 'I suppose you'd be from Leitrim?' The barman was young and cocky. 'Yes. Near enough,' the man said slowly. 'I suppose, now, there wouldn't be too much happening down in Leitrim?' the barman laughed. 'It's peaceable,' the man seemed to agree; 'but not too peaceable. Middlin' peaceable. What you want, like where we're from, across the river. Belcoo. Yes. Middlin' peaceable. What you want. The sky above us.'

168 After school, Manorhamilton, Co. Leitrim

COUNTY SLIGO

Neil Jordan

Memories should be dim, I suppose, but mine turn out to be very dim, confused with old photographs, parental lore and older family friends I've met since then who remember me.

A flock of geese being pursued down a country road by a bawling boy with a stick in his hand, hardly able to walk. That comes from a photograph that I've been shown so often I think of it as memory. Two children being carried up Ben Bulben in a Moses basket – myself and my sister Ursula – an event that took place on the top which I've forgotten, but which my mother must have related to me – hence another half-memory, vicarious this time. The paintings of Jack Yeats, horse fairs, boat-races, were perused so often when I was younger that they too have become like memories. My father moved to Rosses Point during a teachers' strike in the late 1940s, gained employment in a one-teacher school; my mother bore her first two children there. Their early days of marriage seemed as happy as any marriage could be, which is why their memories must have had such potency, and bred a crop of vicarious memories in me. The half-mad neighbour who grabbed Ursula by the hair and held on until she was dragged off by a dozen others. The butterfly collection in my father's school. The local choir he organised, the fiddle-playing, the dances, the winter of the great freeze when a local fisherman walked drunk across the frozen sea and vanished into the ice. The only justification for my claiming them as my own is that they happened, around the time I happened. And so the only genuine memory I can claim is the taste of the Goldgrain biscuits given to me every day by the girl next door.

So by the time the strike ended and my family moved to Dublin and my mother bemoaned the absence of green among the suburban streets, I had managed to acquire by an accident of birth and labour-relations a mythical home, a kind of green world that I would claim as my origin, an alternative to the *petit bourgeois* world I was to grow up in. I would write the word 'Sligo' as my place of birth with a quiet, subversive pride and a sense of belonging to something other than my surroundings. And at times I'd affect a country accent. When we came to visit as a family, some years later, and with the bad-tempered cognisance of all young children I could register enough to truly remember, the realities were more prosaic. A greystone boarding-house in Strand Hill, long summer days spent listening to the rain, wondering when it would clear enough to play, and a long curve of beach and sea, that when it did clear turned out to be too cold to swim in. The sense of belonging remained, though. For some reason, which I have not yet fathomed, it seemed a moral necessity to have come from there. If only to have the luxury of refusing to truly belong. And later, when I came to read the poetry of Yeats, this insistence became a positive boon. 'He stood among a crowd at Dromohair . . .' The fact that I had no real memories of the places was no hindrance to my grabbing them like family heirlooms, utterly possessive and secretly triumphant. Lisadell, Ben Bulben, The Rosses' 'level shore' – the names became intoxicants, as mythological as Samarkand and Valparaiso, yet still they were mine. Joyce, who had

172 The World, Co. Sligo

mythologised the city I lived in, could not hold a candle to this. I swam on Dollymount Strand, took music lessons in Harcourt Street, tried to get served drink in Davy Byrne's, and read him like a medical treatise, a dissection of the utterly familiar.

On my last visit there I was searching for locations for a film, looking for a generic version of the 'big house'. I visited Lisadell with an English crew and drove up the long drive surrounded by poplars, to the plain block of granite facing the water. Every time I'd visited there it had been raining and this time proved no exception. The doors swung open and a gaunt man who seemed like a gardener ushered us inside. A disparate group of tourists was lined up, looking cold and dutifully curious. The last remnants of the family – two sweet, polite old ladies – took us round the bizarre decaying mansion, with its cold, grey granite, damp tapestries and generations of portraits. They themselves lived in a fraction of the building, so the main vista, to the lawns and water, was closed to them. Their brother, I was told, was incarcerated in a home in Sligo, and there had been trouble with the local council, the trees in the estate being sold and cut down against their wishes. The English crew, knowing nothing of the history of the place, shivered, politely incurious, bemused by my own nostalgia. It seemed a most uncomfortable place for two girls in silk kimonos. Poetry, I began to think, must be as false as memory.

174 Selling coats, Co. Laois

COUNTY LAOIS

Sean J. White

My birthplace, the town of Durrow, lies deep in Laois, which itself is deep in the midland plain, the most inland county in Ireland.

Durrow, a small, by Irish standards, market town with its oval of fair-green and its dog-leg of two main streets exiting from it carries its history on its face. The focus of the green is the towered Castle Gate, once the entrance to the 'big house', the Queen Anne mansion of the Flower family, Viscounts Ashbrook and Barons Castle Durrow.

Around the green in elegant, if vernacular, Georgian houses lived estate agents and officers. The servants of the demesne, from head gardener to under kitchen-maid, occupied neat stone houses along the extended streets, occasionally interrupted by the twenty or so shops and pubs that served them, their masters in the castle and the farmers in the surrounding countryside.

My parents kept one of these shops in the side-streets and later a bigger one on the green – hotel, grocery, drapery and bar combined.

The Lords Ashbrook left in the 1920s and the castle became the convent school, my first school. Most of the other estates around the town in its circle of woods also declined, and Durrow went through an extremely bad patch in the 1930s. Not only was there no work for the coachmen, the gardeners, the parlourmaids; the tradesmen also suffered, the two carpenters, the blacksmith, the shoemaker, the saddler and the extended family of tailors widely acclaimed for the hunting coats they made for the gentry. The shopkeepers too suffered and declined in numbers.

Forestry work on the state-acquired estates, relief schemes for the County Council on the roads, occasional and ill-paid work for the hard-pressed local farmers and, if all that failed, catching rabbits or poaching salmon kept the Durrowmen going through the 1930s. The war and work in the munitions factories in England at last relieved the pressure.

Not all Laois was like this declining pocket of the Home Counties, but neither I nor my fellow schoolboys knew this as we were hardly ever more than a bicycle ride from home.

A school inspector with a waxed moustache and a wen on his forehead once awed us with his world travels when he proclaimed 'The Rock of Dunamase is as old, as important, and as beautiful as the Acropolis of Athens.' We had not seen Athens and could not contradict him; in fact we had not seen Dunamase, which was over eighteen miles away.

Now as I drive down the main Cork road, over the Barrow at Monasterevin and through the village of Ballybrittas, a sweet little line of limestone hills rises on the left like the background of an Umbrian landscape. Among them stands the acropolis rock of Dunamase crowned with a shattered castle. I begin to see the school inspector's point. From here it has a strange, ghostly resemblance to the Acropolis. From the

Stradbally side with its drum-tower gates, jagged walls and ruined keep massing above in tier upon tier, it looks more like an Italian hill-town.

The story of Dunamase is a rich composite of people and events and can stand for the story of Laois.

The Celts built a hill fort on the rock as they did on the neighbouring bosky heights. Ptolemy marked it on his map as 'Dunum'. Dermot MacMurrough, King of Leinster, owned it at the time of the Norman invasion and through him it passed to his son-in-law Strongbow and so on in his family to William Marshall, Earl of Pembroke, who built the first proper castle. In turn, it went to William de Braos, ancestor to the Scottish Bruces. A series of royal favourites owned it afterwards: Roger de Mortimer, the Fitzgeralds, Theobald de Verdun and Fulke de Freine, all alternating ownership in the fortunes of war with the local Irish chieftains, the O'Mores. The last occupier was Sir John Parnell, speaker of the Irish Parliament and an ancestor of Charles Stewart Parnell.

As the alternating lordship of Dunamase tells the story of Laois, the view from its ramparts reveals the face of the county. From the main road and especially from the railway, Laois looks flat, with a high proportion of barren bog. From this height you can see that it is a plain almost surrounded by hills. Across the plain to the north and west are the level blue ridges of the Slieve Bloom mountains with bog at their feet and new forestry on their slopes. At one's back at the south-eastern corner is the high plateau of Slieve Margy, part of the Leinster coal ridge. The plain in between, far from being bog, is champaign land with wheatfields and beetfields and hayfields, lots of trees in woody clusters between and in lines along the roads.

Laois owes its well-wooded and watered look, its 'Home Counties' aspect, largely to the fact that it and its neighbour, Offaly, were 'settled' in the mid-sixteenth century to become respectively Queen's and King's counties. On the landscape there are few tangible remains of that early settlement – an occasional high-stacked chimney gable and some fort walls in the county town Portlaoise. The town's old-fashioned vernacular name, Maryborough (pronounced 'Maar-borough'), acknowledges Mary Tudor. After the wars of religion in the seventeenth century Laois got its demesnes and great houses and neat Georgian towns which give it its settled look.

The character of the Laois people, though, does come from that earlier and on the whole peaceful fusion. The settlement of Laois occurred nearly a century before the plantation of Ulster. Maybe the proportion of settlers to natives was more acceptable, or the settlers themselves more congenial, but the mixture seems to have worked. Laois people have a live-and-let-live attitude. They are workaday people, farming and logging, turf-cutting and mining; and in their clean and matter-of-fact towns shop-keeping and making butter and textiles, woodworking and forging metal.

They do have a reputation for being proud. A Laois man, they say, would wear a collar and tie going to the poor-house. Occasionally they have been dissolute. Jonah Barrington, their sharpest memorialist in the eighteenth century, who categorised his gentry friends 'Half-mounted gentlemen, gentlemen every inch of them, gentlemen to the back-bone', repeated their proudest boast: 'every estated gentleman of the Queen's

County was *honoured* by the gout'. Beside Sir Jonah and his gallery of Tudor and Cromwellian adventurers and 'half-sirs', the Dunamase set you might say, one should place the O'Mores, the Dempseys, the Dunnes, the Gaelic originals who fought with, married into, and on the whole lived peacefully with those pushy late arrivals.

Typical of the earlier class was Honest Pat Lalor from Raheen – a substantial farmer, the first Catholic MP for the county since the time of James II, a Justice of the Peace, a notable fighter for the repeal of the Union and unjust tithes. He fathered as diverse and distinguished a family of sons as ever appeared in any county. One was Peter, who led the Australian miners' revolt at the Eureka stockade and lived to be the Conservative Speaker of the Victoria Parliament; another was James Fintan, who took part in the unsuccessful rising in Ireland of 1849 and who gave the peasant ownership movement its potent watchword 'The Land for the People'; Richard was an MP in succession to his father; Thomas was a general in the American Army and Patrick was a famous doctor.

Barringtons and Brophys, O'Mores and Morgans, FitzPatricks, Barons of Upper Ossory who were McGiolla Padhraigs, servants of Saint Patrick, a Gaelic clan of ecclesiastical chieftains, all still occupy and share this centric county, scenically tame but humanly richly eccentric, with few breaches of the peace.

178 Co. Laois

COUNTY DUBLIN

James Plunkett

At the turn of the century Dublin was playing host to an assortment of writers, some of whom were to achieve international reputations of the highest renown, some to win a more modest distinction and others again whose reputations were so diluted by the passing of the years that they have dissolved away into oblivion. Their reactions to their ancient host were as varied as their talents. George Moore, although he could be frosty enough at times, found Dublin agreeable for the most part and spoke of her as a city wandering pleasantly between mountain and sea. James Joyce, who had his indulgent moments also, referred to her affectionately as his 'dear, dirty Dumpling'. Yeats, less tolerant of her posing and posturing and a victim of her incessant gossip, complained bitterly of what he denounced as 'the daily spite of this unmannerly town'. Sean O'Casey blew hot and cold. In one rare, adoring moment he beheld her as a poor but gentle and beautiful girl wrapped in a sober black shawl who had fallen in love with him.

> Stars in the deeps of her eyes are exclaiming
> I carry a bunch of red roses for thee.

But reality returned to O'Casey at the double when the Nationalist die-hards tried to boo one of his plays off the Abbey stage. He stopped to contemplate the three castles which decorated the city's coat of arms: 'Poverty, pain and penance,' (he decided) 'those were the gates of Dublin, its three castles.'

After that he took to referring to her as 'oul snarly gob'.

For anyone growing up in Dublin in the 1930s or 40s it was the 'poverty, pain and penance' bit which seemed to hit her off best. There were tenements in the process of crumbling to bits, filling her worst areas with filth and evil smells. There were the children of their poverty-stricken inhabitants wandering around in tattered clothes and bare feet. Monday mornings saw long queues and pinched faces outside the pawnshops. In contrast to all this were the gracious streets and squares with their tall, well-kept houses which were the heritage of her Georgian era. And brooding over her squalor and grandeur alike, the palpable shadow of her long and troubled history, which stretched from the founding of a small, Viking Age town in the ninth century to the great expansion which began in the seventeenth century and continues even to this day.

For me, it was a good city to grow up in and good to live in. I was born beside the sea which spreads the whole length of the county's eastern border and played on her strands and wandered from a tender age in the mountains that mark her limits to the south. Her squares and her expanses of water made her a place of openness and light and air. Water especially. The Liffey flowed through the city centre and underwent spectacular transformations when the sunset (as it quite frequently does) put on a gala performance and stained water and houses, bridges and rooftops, in a riotous disarray of colour. The Grand Canal, with its tree-lined banks, its stretches of reed-bordered water, its great lock-gates and their silvery, cascading torrents, reflected sky and clouds for double measure. The river Dodder was the shy one. She tiptoed her modest way through quiet haunts and slipped into the sea at Ringsend with little or no fuss.

Beyond Ringsend the great South Wall, a mole about fifteen feet in width, composed of great rust-coloured slabs of granite, continued for three further miles with nothing but the river on one side of it and the sea on the other. Its terminal was a squat lighthouse perched, as it were, in an insubstantial world of changing skies and restless seas. Making the journey to it felt like walking on the water and when one arrived Howth, rising heavenwards at a great distance to the north, and the mountains of Dublin and Wicklow ringing the bay at an even greater distance to the south, hid amid and behind their undulating shapes a network of country lanes and winding boreens which explored the byways of Dublin county, its quieter retreats of green fields or brown bogland and rock-strewn mountain streams.

Oliver Cromwell had landed at Ringsend in 1646 with an army of 8,000 foot and 4,000 horse plus a train of battering guns. With these he proceeded to spread terror throughout the length and breadth of the country. Centuries before him the Vikings landed on the same stretch of the river and built a settlement there to provide a jumping-off ground for their raids inland, and later to provide a town for marketing and trading. They were followed in turn by the Norman and then by the English. Louis MacNeice in an oft-quoted poem summed up the ancestry of the city:

> Fort of the Dane
> Garrison of the Saxon
> Augustan capital
> of a Gaelic Nation

Of the early churches, St Patrick's Cathedral is the one which knitted itself most closely into the unfolding of the city of Dublin's history. The citizens are said to have built the first little church there in the fifth century to mark the visit of St Patrick to the spot and his miraculous provision of a well of sparkling water to replace the brackish and foul-tasting stuff they had been forced to put up with until then. Cromwell, it is said, stabled his horses in it and the gloomy Dean, the great Jonathan Swift, became a champion of the city's poor and despised. They adored the Dean of St Patrick's. Once, when a noisy mob had gathered at the cathedral to await an eclipse of the moon, they dispersed without difficulty when a message was passed out to them to say that it had been postponed on the Dean's instructions.

Phoenix Park is another precious asset of the city which became a haunt of childhood. Its 1,752 acres of open parkland were secured in the seventeenth century for the citizens by the Duke of Ormonde, who had to cross swords with the Duchess of Cleveland over it. She was demanding it from Charles II as a reward for services rendered. When Ormonde won the day she expressed the hope of living to see him hanged. Ormonde, in reply, confessed it to be his deepest wish that he would live long enough to see her old.

But wit and repartee and the cutting edge of the tongue have always held a prominent place in Dublin's history and reputation. I am reminded of Dublin Castle, which was

181 Dublin City, Co. Dublin

182 Shopkeeper, Dublin

begun on the instructions of King John in the thirteenth century to keep the native clans in control. With the passing of time it became the principal seat of British rule in Ireland and was held generally in disaffection by the citizenry, who had little faith in the impartiality of its administration. This was given expression in a popular verse of the time which was written when a statue representing Justice was put in place on top of the Castle's Cork Hill Gate:

> The statue of Justice
> Mark well her station
> Her face to the Castle
> Her arse to the Nation

That speaks unmistakably in the accents of dear old dirty Dumpling.

184 First couple, Dublin

185 Single man, Dublin

186 Second couple, Ballymun, Dublin

187 Ballymun, Dublin

188 Autumn, Co. Kerry

COUNTY KERRY

Brendan Kennelly

There are many people who say that Kerry is the most beautiful county in Ireland and if you ask any Kerryman his opinion on this matter he'll inform you without hesitation that these people could be right or they could be wrong. He'll offer you this nugget of non-information with the air of a man who is sharing with you a revelation he has kept secret from the rest of the world until now, because the rest of the world is sadly lacking in your special brand of sensitivity and intelligence, and isn't it great that he has finally met someone he can trust with his secret? A Kerryman will make you feel good in spite of yourself. He'll touch your heart like the air of one of those divine days in Banna Strand or Ballybunion or Killarney or Dingle. For one blissful moment, he'll be your sun and moon, your warm air and your cool light rain of summer because there's only the loan of us there and we might as well be laughing as crying and we'll get nothing for complaining and God loves a smiling face and will you stand back and *look* at yourself – why, the years are running off you like water off a duck's back, it's getting younger you are like the angels guarding the children, you're turning out to be the spitting image of your father, and won't you sit down there in the chair near the window, take the weight off your legs, rest the bones, I'm just making a pot of tea, or would you prefer an honest shot of Jameson without the insult of water in it?

Throughout the length and breadth of Ireland, Kerry is known as 'the Kingdom'. Sometimes I think it is a kingdom of talkers. At any time of the year the Kerry people are ready to talk the night into morning, sorrow into joy, indifference into passion. Kerry is a kingdom of gossip.

I once heard an old priest describe gossip as a holy and healthy thing because it showed you had a vigorous interest in your neighbour's life and affairs, so vigorous, in fact, that the neighbour could rest assured that if he lived alone and died of a sudden the rats wouldn't have time to get at him because everyone around him would be peeking through his window wondering why he wasn't out trying to borrow the sports pages of yesterday's *Irish Independent*. There must be something wrong with the poor mean oul bastard if he's not out and about looking for something for nothing; come on up to the house, lads, and we'll see if he's alive or dead or in bed with the blue flu!

And of course it would have to be the sports pages. There are two religions in Kerry – Roman Catholicism and Gaelic football. Of the two, Catholicism is dominant for a large part of the year; but once the Munster Final comes in June or July there is a noticeable change in the spiritual atmosphere; football and endless implacable analysis of football and footballers take over. If you want to talk about world wars or bombs or progress or tourism or the state of the economy you will not be able to do so in Kerry, at that time of the year. The real questions are: Will we bate Cork? Is the midfield a bit shaky? Will Jacko's ankle be better in time? What's the referee like? Are the Cork lads going to cut up rough? Jesus, they're terrible when they're rough, they'd kick their mothers out of the chapel.

190 On the road to Kenmare, Co. Kerry

191 Derrynasaggart Mountains, Co. Kerry

192 Clouds opening, Co. Kerry

I had the privilege of growing up in a village pub in Kerry; and I can honestly say that nowhere in the world have I heard the kind of animated talk I've heard there. Most of this talk was, and is, about football. These men in the pub, endless pints of Guinness in their fists, talk of style, rhythm, fielding, running, catching, free-kicking, goals and points with a kind of relentless attention and detail that makes you listen. Even to the rare non-follower of football the talk is interesting, not for the content, but for the tone of authentic knowledge and fierce enthusiasm.

Most impressive of all, however, is the *memory* of these talkers. It is a long memory and it pertains to matters other than football: to the Civil War, for example, or to feuds between neighbours; to bastardy in families or trouble over land or rights of way through certain fields. There is a lot of trouble over land. One of the most powerful Irish plays, *The Field* by John B. Keane, who owns a pub in Listowel, deals with this recurring problem. It is a powerful and moving drama.

Drama: that is the word that best describes both the landscape and the lives of the people who inhabit this most beautiful kingdom. It is this *dramatic* character, riddled with moods and changes, that draws visitors back to Kerry year after year. The poems and stories of the people are intensely dramatic; they reach back to the Famine, they speak and sing of hunger, deprivation, poverty, sickness, emigration, death. But they also sing and speak of love, friendship, endurance, victory, and always, unfailingly, of the heroic footballers preserved for ever in the long memory of song.

A free to Kerry, Con Brosnan took it
With steady foot and unerring aim;
He scored the point and again we led them,
'Twas the final score of a hard-fought game.

Hats off to Brosnan, our midfield wonder,
He's *par excellence* in feet and hands.
O where's the man can pull down the number
Of Kerry's idol from Newtownsandes?

Today, Kerry is a relatively prosperous part of Ireland, though the county is being badly hit by emigration, due to government cut-backs. But wherever they go, Kerry people take Kerry with them. I have met them in places all over the world and it always does my heart good to see them and talk with them. They'll come up to you in a bar in Boston or London or Paris or Brussels and, well, there's only one topic of conversation: Kerry. The talk is usually not sentimental; it is marked rather by a special blend of affection and pride. Sometimes it is critical, but rarely bitter. And there is always the resolution, spoken or unspoken, to go back. This is entirely understandable because once Kerry gets into your blood it is there forever. It is a heart's bundle of dramatic images, a living presence of talkers, singers, dancers, footballers, a picture of festivities at the Rose of Tralee Week, Listowel and Killarney Races, Puck Fair in Killorglin, Writers' Week in Listowel, the Munster Final and then, with God's help, on to the All-Ireland where we can meet and beat Dublin or anyone. But, above all, Kerry is its people with their long memories and quick tempers and their words showering over you in a rain of profuse delight. It's good to see you, Brendan. O God but you're getting fat like your father. Are you off the whiskey or would you care for a drop? Good to see you. Come in, come in. You're welcome, welcome.

195 Four in the morning, on the Cork border, Co. Kerry

196 Mist over the mountains and lakes, Killarney, Co. Kerry

198 Bus shelter, Co. Wexford

COUNTY WEXFORD

John Banville

Wexford is not there. It began to fade twenty-five years ago when I left the place and went to search for life. Each time I returned it was all a little paler, a little more transparent, everything miniature and quaint. My visits too contracted, while the lapses between them grew. The farther afield I travelled, the farther it all diminished behind me, like the cosmonaut Kelvin's home at the end of Tarkovsky's *Solaris*, a tiny patch of russet and green adrift in the sea of remembrance. Then one summer six or seven years ago it disappeared finally, the whole kit and boodle, when I went there for a holiday with my wife and sons: to be a holiday-maker in the place where you were born is to achieve a melancholy dominion over it. There was a Wexford still, identical with the one I had known, and utterly different. My wife showed me around. 'Look how lovely it is, look what you missed, all those years!' I was not fooled. 'It's Wexford, all right,' I said, 'but it's not Wexford.' I could see the brush-strokes, the cleverly-placed mirrors, could detect the sewing in the seams.

And of course it was, is, will be, lovely. (Whatever that may mean, for what can a place be but itself?) Mine was a charmed childhood, in the midst of fields.

There stays for us perhaps a tree on a hillside, which daily we can take into our vision.

There is a certain path, at the foot of a small hill, with three trees, where once, one surreptitious sunny day in June, I saw a cuckoo; we looked at each other, bird and boy, up and down, and the breeze hissed in the high leaves. There is a garage on the docks in New Ross outside which I sat one late-autumn night in a Morris Oxford motor car (smell of leather and hot oil) while my Uncle Tom was inside talking to a man and I sobbed quietly to myself for no reason other than that the river was black and the cobbles were slimed with moonlight and a tin sign was creaking in the wind. There is a grey warm muggy morning in Rosslare Strand, the sea strangely flat and high, like the humped back of a vast mild beast, and my brother and his friends playing ball, and I among them, a child and condescended to and happy.

The small hushed waves' repeated fresh collapse

This is the geography of memory; of imagination; these are the sacred images, the icons of the heart.

What kind of Irish place-name would have an 'x' in it?

I was born in the town of Wexford, in a place called The Faythe (Irish *Faithe*, pronounced 'faha'), a narrow isosceles tapering towards the Rosslare road, with cherry-blossom trees that shed pink blizzards in the first May winds, and a green, circular horse-trough surmounted by a painted metal swan. A *faithe* was in ancient times a sort of parade-ground for soldiery, and for a while I was much taken with the image of great gaunt heroes, Fionn's men, clattering up and down our street, stamping and bellowing, reeking of blood and pelts and iron. It was at Wexford that the Normans first landed, in the twelfth century, Henry II's robber barons. I used to walk with my mother on Banna Strand, and imagine the keels grating on that gravelled shore to inaugurate eight hundred years of troubles. The thought of the lemon sponge cake awaiting me at home for my tea was far more vivid.

I had, nor have, none of that loyalty to county which is a characteristic of the Irish. To me, when I lived there, the notion of 'Wexford', and all that the name was supposed to imply, was faintly risible. It was long after I had left that I realised how deeply I was rooted in the place, or how deeply it was rooted in me. All the landscapes of my books are in some way imbued with wexfordness, even when they are supposed to be modern Greece, or medieval Prussia. When I needed to paint a picture of Copernicus's Torun or Kepler's Weilderstadt, it was Wexford that I conjured up. Now, when a reader tells me how well I captured the Swabia of the seventeenth century, I smile politely, and hear a ghostly Wexford weasel-voice saying, *Oh, him? – sure, I knew his oul fella.*

I once went to Wexford during the opera festival to give a reading from my work and not a single soul turned up. I felt more a grim sense of vindication than anything else. Since then, the town and I have made it up, and I have found some of my best audiences there. All the same . . .

My sister lives there now, that is my last real link with the place. Sometimes, when I visit her, I venture down the Main Street, where I used to idle as a boy, trembling with impatience and scorn. I hardly know anyone: a new generation has taken over. Is it an illusion, or are they brighter, happier, more at ease here than I could ever have been? Now and then I spot a known face being worn, inexplicably, by someone impossibly young, then I realise it is not a schoolfriend I am seeing, but a schoolfriend's son.

The Main Street I can manage, but I would not now have the courage to walk up The Faythe any more, or sit in the back row of the Abbey Cinema, or stand on the pitted courts of Melrose Tennis Club (does it still exist?), or wander through the fields that we knew as the Rocks, where one gold and green evening I walked with my parents, and my mother picked bluebells and my father found a bird's nest, and the dog barked, and a thrush sang thickly, and the late sunlight seemed a haze of pure happiness. Do I misremember? Do I invent? Is it Wexford, or a Wexford I have created? What does it matter. Something is there.

201 Collecting for charity, Co. Wexford

202 Unemployed man, Naas, Co. Kildare

COUNTY KILDARE

Aidan Higgins

I remember it in the time of paraffin lamps, anthracite, sago, Bird's Custard, farthings, wetted coke, servants, triple-layer buns from Boland's delivery van, frog-spawn and tadpoles wriggling in the pond at the edge of the Crooked Meadow, cruel hare-coursing, twists of hard-boiled sweeties in paper bags, Findlater's men from Dublin, Wild Woodbines in open-end packets of five for twopence halfpenny, a mad dog running circles in a field, myself sick and giddy from the first tobacco, the PP's alarming *Diktat* from the pulpit on Sundays, pea-picking, mushrooming in Mangan's field; the stink of the convent class, the musty smell of nuns, the provenance of sin, a writhing serpent impaled on the Patriarch's crozier, the purple-shrouded statues of Holy Week, the whispering at Confession. In a stationary, dull, provincial society that would never change – but change it did, and drastically, in my absence.

Away from the *Kindschaft* of Crunchies and Dev's Snots (a cone-shaped chocolate whirl with whipped cream) and Bulls' Eyes and Peggy's Leg, liquorice twists, fizzy sherbet, servants churning in the chill dairy, oak tubs for the butter pats, bluebottles buzzing in the larder and a snipe rotting on a hook, cat-stench behind the mangle, sheets airing on the bleach-green, cows calving and mares foaling and stallions mounting and sows farrowing and ewes lambing and shit flying and priests praying and nuns walking with pinched lips between cypress trees on the convent avenue and the big girls tittering and hay-bogies on the by-roads and corncrakes in the meadow and steamrollers stinking and two-score Collegiate girls in blue uniforms rounding Brady's corner and their teachers with long thin disobliging Anglican horse-faces, and Satan dining in Castletown.

Not to mention the bridles and winkers, saddles and britching, mallet and teaser, the furriers and the harness-makers, a rabbit choking in a snare, the furnaces stoked, the bank manager appeased, the River Liffey flowing through Killadoon Wood, everything in its proper place. Pitch-and-toss at the crossroads after Sunday Mass, and the Bogeyman lurking in the cellar with the arrowheads and the mouldy masks, the suicide in the quarry said to be depthless, and the headstones in the graveyard, and the soldiers firing volleys over the open grave, the patriot interred. In the late 1950s the tractors arrived and the horses went and with them the old days. But where did all the cobblers go?

Hall's Ireland (1841) of pre-Famine days divides Kildare into the baronies of Carbery, Clane-Connell, Ikeathy and Oughterany, Kilcullen, Kilkea and Moone, East Narragh and Rheban, West Narragh and Rheban, East Ophaly, West Ophaly, North and South Naas and North and South Salt. Springfield, bought by my progenitor from old Mrs Warren, was one of the big houses of North Salt, along with Windgates, Griffinrath, Ballynakill, Kippanour, Corbally, Possackstown, Marley Abbey where the Dean broke with Esther Vanhomrigh – then it became the property of Lady Gregory and, later on, the brothers of St John of God cared for the mentally ill there. In 1776 Arthur Young passed through Celbridge, later again Virginia Woolf. The chronically impecunious young James Joyce walked twelve miles from Dublin, trying to raise a loan, walked home disappointed.

Robert Lowell lived in Castletown for a time in the 1960s, visited by the precociously gifted young poet Heaney. Madame Popoff the Russian lady lived over at St Woolstans.

Up in the foothills stood Peamount Sanatorium for consumptives and Baldonnel Aerodrome from where Lysanders, Avro Ansons and Tiger Moths flew up like gnats, though the Irish Air Force (motto: Small But Fierce) never went to war, Ireland being neutral, Dev would not surrender the ports.

When Dorniers and Heinkels flew over Kildare, thrown off course by the RAF, these old-timers hid in the clouds. Interned in the Curragh camp but let out for the day, RAF and Luftwaffe pilots drank in the Buttery Bar of the Shelbourne Hotel and called for Messerschmidt cocktails, while the foe called for Spitfires and Hurricanes, twirling their moustaches.

But mostly I recall those prolonged summer twilights, the piling-up of brilliantly white cirro-cumulus, the frisky air of the Liffey valley, hard winter frosts with a bone in the ground, a side of roast beef sliced and re-heated in the kitchen oven for my young brother and myself after school with the nuns. My father's best suit was warmed up in the oven and carried upstairs to the steamy bathroom by Lizzy Bolger our maid. Buckets of boiling water for the bath; and after long immersion my father stood in clean flannel combinations and shaved himself carefully with a cut-throat razor. Then the dressing, the application of cologne and powder, Brylcreem applied with the palms of both hands and worked in with *two* hairbrushes, quiff parted in the middle like Mandrake the Magician in the *Evening Mail* strip. The high sheen on his fine black leather pointy shoes would dazzle you; dressy, he stopped just short of spats, a Malacca cane.

Then the silken display handkerchief erupting from the breast pocket, the 'shooting' of cufflinks, the swift ball of malt before setting out on foot for Hazelhatch Station three miles away, for the Overland and then the Rover had no licence, my father bribing the guards with loads of wood, obliged to walk through the village 'in case they might be out'.

Around us the high plantation, the shrubbery, the two gate-lodges, in a near-Protestant style of reclusiveness. Herds of cattle with dungy hindquarters were driven by on the road by herdsmen in equally dungy wellingtons, from as far afield as Enfield, Birr and Edenderry, *en route* for embarkation at the Dublin docks to the abattoirs and glue factories over the water. Flocks of sheep followed with their lambs baa-ing piteously. Turf carts moved by night from the Bog of Allen.

I recall: flayed meat hung on great hooks outside the nasty butcher's, whole sides of beef; inverted porkers split up the middle bled from their snouts into the sawdust, shamelessly nude. My father tried everything with his long nose before putting it into his mouth, crossing his legs, bolting it down like a dog.

All has changed now, as in Ithaca. When I revisited the old homestead after a lapse of twenty years or more I found it all changed, and yet the same. To return to childhood haunts is to retreat into a land which has become unreal and 'hermetically disturbing'. I must have read that somewhere; it strikes a chord. A paler shade of grey prevails there.

How strange is the land! Our racial history – the past – seems unreal and disturbing; for time has stopped there in an anxious, boundless limbo. Newbridge has moved miles westward; no horses in the fields but you feel their presence everywhere, an unhorsed stable-lad limps home near Kilcock. No poultry in the back yards, no washing on the line, TV aerials over every house, the natives have moved indoors. Great power pylons march across Kildare, released from Ardnacrusha in County Clare.

The *Evening Standard* press photographer John Minihan, born in Athy where nine cemeteries accommodate a population of under 5,000 souls, studied the technique of the American photographer Curtis, who had recorded the degradation of the North American Indians, another unfortunate race deprived of its lands, tenure, rights, water, gods, all. Minihan photographed the wake of Katy Tyrrell in 1977, almost the last wake in Ireland, as if there could ever be such an ending – for we will never stop waking our dead. The defunct Leinsterwoman laid out between starched sheets – the emblematic scapulars and holy icons and relics looked barbaric – might have passed for a Mohawk squaw.

Flat, unaccented speech distinguishes the men of the Kildare plains, the short-grass county with its bog-asphodel and killer weed, fieldmice in the dandelions. They cannot allow their hopes to rise too high, for history has branded them as malcontents. St Brigid is blushing on her pedestal, a coffin rests on trestles at the rear of the church, near baby Jesus sprawled in the straw.

All hidden and secluded places pleased me: under the linen table-cloth, up the yew tree, in the shrubbery, in the plantation, in Killadoon Wood, that shadowy evanescent Protestant place hidden behind estate walls topped with the necks of broken Guinness bottles. I felt uneasy for my life and was apprehensive and superstitious as a cave-woman's brat before history was recorded or anything had a name.

In a red flood the Liffey poured into Castletown demesne by Christ Church on the site of Conolly's kennels, flowing purposefully on into Protestant land. Now Anna Liffey had become a Protestant river, flowing dark brown with its sunken weeds streaming bold as banners; along its banks strutted cock pheasants and Protestants with grey faces, ignoring the black rabbits skipping about; until it emerged on the far side as a Catholic river again, full of abandoned things, bicycle-frames and waterlogged cardboard boxes and animal skulls, horsehair stuffing from a broken sofa; to flow on towards Lucan and the dog-track at Chapelizod and Dublin and the brewery and all the bridges and then Ringsend and the sea.

As a lad I was much given to melancholy bucolic reverie, sunk in apathy and sloth, never in the best of health, moving around in a dream, chronically worried. Great gaps yawned in our troubled history (nothing between the departure of the Vikings and the arrival of Cromwell and his butchers; nothing between the sinking of the *Lusitania* and Dev's most undiplomatic message of condolence to the German people on the death of Hitler ⇥ this on behalf of the Irish people into whose collective heart he claimed to see; and between the passing of Poyning's Law and the Wyndham Act of 1903, nothing) and in me too a small gap yawned.

The 'humorous' national magazine *Dublin Opinion* liked to show our leaders in as flattering a light as possible: archly comic figures in a cock-shy at some country fête, perhaps in Maynooth. Dev in a long black overcoat, Aiken, the wily Lemass, Minister of External Affairs Boland, wee Willie Cosgrave and the amiable gnome Alfie Byrne, Lord Mayor of Dublin, all with vaudeville moustaches, mutton-chop whiskers, all droll, dotes, toys you could take to bed; at all events, none were to be taken seriously.

Irish politics, like Roman Catholicism, gave off an antiseptic carbolic smell of Lifebuoy soap. A rustic functional cleanliness obtained, though our politics as such seemed to be more concerned with the dead than with the living, a washing of corpses in the morgue. Effigies hunched up in the niches of Catholic graveyards were the true past, the long-dead ones staring back at the living with shocked, round, afflicted stone eyes.

When did you last see a woman wringing her hands? or an old fellow wearing yellow bicycle clips? or greyhounds on the leash? or the inextinguishable fires of wayside itinerants with washing on bushes, they themselves (the great unwashed) none too clean?

A pasty-faced youth with long greasy black hair and black leather jacket walks in a menacing way through Naas in the rain, believing himself to be the zombie Michael Jackson. He belongs to the gross neon-lit world, Nás na Rí, the old assembly-place of the kings, immersed in the lurid atmosphere of unbridled dream, juke-boxes blaring. Modern Ireland, gone to hell, has become a sort of Ready-Made America, with shopping malls, McDonald's, video shops open on Sunday. Wearing baseball caps, some dumb logo on their jogging suits, the bostoons are getting smart, with Yankee-style push and affrontery ('Have a nice day!'), ordering Budweiser; the compelling pull of the soda-pop stall. Auspicious hours. In the old days, say fifty years ago, a tailor could run you up a good Dugdale suit of navy blue serge for less than three quid. Four quid for two tons of coal —

Oh great just Divinity! *DUGdale* did I hear? No safe houses then, no protection rackets; no arms dumps, no Provo bars or bordellos; no choler of the envenomed ones, that blood brotherhood, men of darkness, sanguinivorous bugaboos vain of their power yet 'ignorant as durt'.

207 Unemployed man in kitchen, Naas, Co. Kildare

208 Young unemployed man in kitchen, Athlone, Co. Westmeath

COUNTY WESTMEATH

Dermot Healy

The doctor strolls into the bedroom and taps my mother's stomach. 'You're not ready yet, ma'am,' he says to her. 'Be the holy,' she trustingly replies. 'That woman of yours will be some hours yet,' he tells my father on the porch. He studies the low Finea sky. 'You'll find me in Fitz's.' My father sits on a chair at the bottom of the bed. My mother has a slight crossing of the eye, and because she hasn't her glasses on she looks the more vulnerable. He has had water boiling downstairs all day. The November night goes on. Some time later she goes into labour again. My father gets the doctor from the pub. He looks at her stomach, counts the intervals between her heaves, then says 'Move over!' My mother does. He unlaces his shoes and gets in beside her. 'Call me, ma'am, when you're ready,' he says and falls into a drunken sleep. My father is waiting patiently outside on the stairs. Time passes. The snores carry to him. Eventually he turns the handle and peers into the low-ceilinged room. He can't believe his eyes. 'Jack,' she whispers, 'get Mary Sheridan, do.' He brings Mary Sheridan back on the bar of his bike. The tilly-lamps flare. At three in the morning Mary delivers the child. Whether the doctor woke, I don't know.

(Until recently I believed this was how I was born. In fact, all this took place in a neighbour's house up the road and it was my mother, not Mary, who arrived as midwife.)

Finea sits on the river Inny which runs between Lough Sheelin and Lough Kinale under a mighty bridge that divides Cavan from Westmeath. Sheelin, troubled now, was then a powerful, whitewashed, lustrous lake. But Kinale was always magical and dark. The arches under the bridge are caves where rain is always seeping. Tom Keogh drives cattle past to drink. Eels slither by. A family keeps eel-boxes up-river and you can peer through the holes to see them, all moist and black and uncoiling. They are more dangerous than a can of worms. Their camouflage is weed and shadow. Sonny Coyle cuts the heads off the eels on the step of his house. Cats carry them away in their teeth with tough growls. Trout skate mid-water in the shallows, watch our worms approach, then skip out of the way. Trout are aristocrats. They have two seasons – before the mayfly and after the mayfly. Meanwhile, we bake perch in a stone fire under the bushes in Fitzsimon's field, and eat them, bones and all. Oilskinned fishermen from abroad steady each other as they climb the stone walls. We swim in the river, boys and girls, tall cold water to our necks. Girls were never so white as then. Neither were we. One day the cows ate the girls' clothes and they had to go to the village in their knickers. On the east side of Kinale the water is covered with unexplained layers of dry sifting yellow reeds. On the west whispering acres of them grow, taut and green.

When my mother was seven she walked into the lower pub to get mints. Behind the shop counter was the woman of the house. Behind the bar counter was the man,

210 Don't Be Cruel, Athlone, Co. Westmeath

without a stitch on him. He had a black umbrella over his head. 'Why?' I asked my mother. 'To get his own back on his wife,' she told me, pressing her hands into her lap, then seconds later, slapping her knees. 'The cursed drink,' she added, shaking her head at what memory will do.

It's a thunderstorm. Uncle Tom from England, who bets on horses, and his wife Bridgie, my mother's sister, are in the boat. My father is at the oars. We've been fishing Kinale pike. Every so often Uncle Tom cries out, 'Bloody hell, did you see that, Jack?' Then the storm breaks. And in the uproar my father loses an oar. He tries paddling after it, but a dark mist falls. We could see nothing. Then it grows clear as day. My father's face lights up like a stranger's. The rumble seems to start under water. Then the awesome crack. Uncle Tom is wearing a straw hat. I sit between my father's legs which are braced firmly against the struts. We go round in circles. Bridgie starts oaring with Tom's hat. 'Blessed God,' says my father. We are out there for hours. Then the keel softly parts the reeds. Tom whistles a Cockney air. My father stands at the bow pushing us forward with the remaining oar. We are in the reeds for hours. I will never forget their sound. And the sky cracking over. At last we touch land. All in the boat, except me, are dead.

My father is buried in Castletown graveyard. He was a Roscommon man from Elphin. He's in a grave with all the Slacks, my mother's family. Her father, mother, grand-aunt. He loved Finea. Guard Healy. He kept an acre of cabbages and potatoes which he divided with the village. We were out in the winter unearthing a few spuds from the pit, which was covered with old straw and turf, when suddenly a rat leaped out. He pinned him to the earth with the prong of a grape. We were out at Derrycrave Bog. When the cart was turning, one of its wheels slipped into a bog-hole. The ass reared. I slid along the plank. The cart lurched. The ass's eyes and my father's eyes were wild. But they got it righted. The wet clunk of the shovels begins. I find wild bilberries. We start tossing. Then someone sights her coming. Mammy is coming. She's coming the straight bog-road that leads to Castlepollard. Whatever she's carrying in one hand is wrapped in white linen. In the other hand she dangles a pail of buttermilk. When she reaches us at last we sit around on the dry sods. Westmeath is relaxing all round us. Each Monday she goes to Ballywillan station to get the train to Cavan for the fair-day of a Tuesday. The mother's side has a bakery and restaurant there. So he comes up early from the station to put us to bed. Then he goes back out for a drink. I am amazed at all the sounds of the village. Charlie Clavin's half-door. Charlie Clavin's old Ford. The bicycle repairman still at work. A swan. Eventually, I pick his step out from the others at closing time. He slips the catch. Coughs. Touches a chair. Leaves his shoes aside. I prepare. He comes into the room quietly and undresses. Gets in beside me. There's only the sound of the ivy. I pretend to be sleeping. Then, first I breathe in the sweet smell of the Guinness. Then I wait for it. Soon the match flares up. The cigarette glows. I watch him mesmerised. His satisfaction is entire.

At the green pump there is a monument raised to 'Myles the Slasher'. On the first of August they used hold a parade in honour of him. He belonged to the Breifne O'Reillys and defended Westmeath against the enemy. In the struggle both his arms were chopped off. But he continued to fight on to the last with a sword gripped between his teeth. In fact, the sword had penetrated both his cheeks. It was an enemy sword, but he clamped his teeth on it and fought valiantly on. I know the spot he fell. It was on the Westmeath side, in a little alcove. There's a song by Percy French called *Come Back Paddy Reilly to Ballyjamesduff* which goes:

Just turn to the left at the Bridge of Finea
And stop when half-way to Cootehill.

But it can't be done. No matter how you try you can't turn left unless you go up Bullasheer Lane, which leads eventually to the banks of floating reeds. Some make an argument for the Carrick road. But it's all cod. And that's how I found writers not only make up things, but get things wrong as well. It was much later that I found Myles the Slasher never stood on the bridge at all. Historians now say he was off fighting the King of Spain. But the monument to fiction still stands outside Kit Daly's door. (And my mother presently lives in Cootehill.) That's how it's done. Call it by another name, and people it with souls from another world.

Joe and Eileen are having another row on the doorstep of their galvanised house. I used love to sit in there and listen to the rain with the chaos all round me. When his parents argue Tadhg gets dizzy. Once, Uncle Seamus gave him cigarettes and he got sick. He stood in the village like a clocking hen because he was afraid to go home. At last he went down to Sheridan's house. Old Mrs Sheridan had taken to the bed. She used to sleep all day and read almanacs and American magazines by night. So Tadhg went past the two old Sheridan sisters who were sitting by the kitchen range and went on into their mother's room. He climbed into bed beside her and fell asleep, and got up when he felt better. When he appeared in the kitchen Biddy asked, 'Where are you coming from?' 'I got in behind your mother,' answered Tadhg, 'because I was too sick to go home.' 'Glory be,' said Sissy. The old lady had never found him in her bed. Like our neighbour hardly cared when the doctor climbed into hers. The village was always sleeping around. Tadhg was a great traveller, my father maintained, but not as great as his father Joe. For the day that they were arguing on the step Joe cracked twelve matches and when they were lit he shoved them into Eileen's face. 'Matches,' I asked the mother. 'Matches,' she nodded. Eileen ran to get the guards. My father was on duty. When he came up there was no sign of Joe. They checked Ballywillan for fear he was trying to get the train to Mullingar. But he was not to be found. He'd taken with him the only loaf of bread in the house and a pot of jam. 'The fecking haverel,' shouted Eileen. 'Easy,' said my father, but she was demented. Joe was gone the following day, and the day after that, and the day after that again. On the fourth morning she was sitting having her breakfast, and enjoying his absence, when a stone dropped onto her plate from a hole in the ceiling. It was Joe dropped that stone. His bread had run out and he was above in the rafters mad with the hunger. The sight of her eating below was the last straw. Then he came down. Tadhg made for our house.

I mind to see a man hanging from a tree. Maybe I didn't see a man but heard it from my mother. But I know it happened during Mass and I saw the rope. I can see the noose swinging in behind the repair shop where all the bicycles stood – upside-down, sideways, without pedals, without wheels, with warped spokes, saddleless. Then one day all the men in the village went to Aden. My brother, educated in Multyfarnham, went with them. Aden did for Finea what Scotland did for Donegal. Each mantelpiece had a photograph resting against the wall of men in shorts. My sister falls off a hayshifter, down between the shafts and under the horses' hooves. I am sitting holding tight to the hay-rope on the top of the cock. She is very pale. It gave everyone a fright. A boy ran in front of a car and was knocked out. The petrified driver ran for the guards. When my father came up the village it was me he found lying there.

The man who rose the umbrella over his naked body died naked sitting on a smothered pig. And in the galvanised house Tadgh was sick again with the flu and couldn't make it to the evening devotions that began Lent. So, when his parents appeared back, he called from his sickbed, 'What are the regulations?' – for fear some new and finer penance might have been introduced. Joe stuck his head round the door and said, 'There's no fast for lunatics.' There were as many wonders in Finea as there were in Fore up the road where dead monks strolled round at night and water flowed uphill, and as many squinting windows as there were in Devlin where Brinsley McNamara wrote *The Valley of the Squinting Windows*. There were many voices to record Westmeath – Goldsmith, Leo Daly, Lord Longford, Conleth Ellis, John Broderick, Desmond Egan, Patrick O'Farrell. The Lilliput Press. Paddy Graham, painter. And it was to a small business in Mullingar that Joyce dispatched Bloom's estranged daughter in a brief, haunting aside. Joyce too succumbed to the scourge of the broken family, and it was to the same town that he had once come to sing, when singing was his forte, that he sent the fictional Millie, as years later Ireland would send their unmarried mothers to Castlepollard. He must have thought that County Westmeath had about it that sense of separation, of inwardness, of dullness even, necessary to portray a guilt over unfinished things. For it is the half-way house between the magic realism of the West and the bustling consciousness of the East. Like a childhood memory that won't budge.

When I was three I ate a pound of homemade butter. I mind to see it sitting in a dish come from Granard. It looked delicious. I took a long time eating it, thinking of things. The window was behind me, the table in front of me, and the turf-fireplace to the left. On the window opposite, the radio sat forever tuned to Athlone, the centre of Ireland. It was the radio prompted me to eat the butter. Its various voices brought hunger on. You knew dinner-time and breakfast-time by the timbre of the voice broadcasting. 'Walton's' brought men in from the fields. But who was talking the day I ate the butter I'd love to know. When my mother came back I was puking furiously – Doctor Galligan told my mother that I was over-active. 'Give him things to do,' he advised. She put me to bring in a few sods of turf from the shed to the back door. Then she forgot all about me. When eventually she opened the back door turf fell in. I had brought half the winter stack across the yard, followed by the hens. And was still bringing more. And would have continued to this very day if she hadn't stopped me. It was grand relaxed work. All the Westmeath people are very relaxed if they are doing something useful and extraordinary. The best land is down by stately Mullingar. They say 'Beef to the heel like a Mullingar heifer.' Round Church Island on Sheelin Counties Meath (the half-sister), Cavan and Westmeath meet for a dip. Jim Keogh oars by with three English fishermen. Uncle Seamus comes in the back door with three duck. He drives a sweet van through Westmeath. Once when he slipped a disc in his spine I got to deliver with him. Street, Coole, Bunbrosna. Oatfields, Liquorice Allsorts, Flash bars. All the grown-ups had bad teeth. The children had teeth like white mice. There's a wake up the road. They dress the corpse in a bob-tail coat and hard hat. During the celebrations the mourning house is burned to the ground, but they save the corpse and sit him in a ditch till morning for the hearse to take him while they follow on bicycles. 'Up Idiot Street,' says Mary Ellen Flynn. I fall in love with Sheila Ledwidge whose father owns the post office. My cousins from England drive the local boys mad.

It's night-time and I can hear voices on the path. I look down from the window to see my father and two other men. They're carrying lamps and torches. A pike the length of the path is stretched out. I find later he was a record forty-four pounds. One man takes a saw and cuts the fish in three. What part we got, I don't know. They had been out shooting in Kinale when this big pike, like a whale, began following them. When they came in he was still with them. So they shot him. Kinale is still the best pike lake in Europe. The Germans know that. It has the strangest underwater you have ever seen. The bottom one minute is sandy and only a couple of feet away. Then it's green and swirling and six feet away. And then with a race to the heart you row over nothing. That nothingness can scare people. I've known a man in the horrors head for shore when it happened. That stretch of water was too much for him. I've found that nothingness in my dreams. And in my love affairs. When you feel trapped in someone else's memory. Out of its depths recently came a bible-stand, which now sits proudly in the Dublin Museum. The forest of reeds, the snipe, Brian McHugh's kitchen, and the mouth of the river where the girls showed us their private parts if we would show ours and we did and everything were studied very closely. And it can still bring a tremor to the voice. There were pissing competitions. And other things.

My mother stands in the kitchen singing in a voice popular when she was young (a scatter of notes on thin ice) and in words contriving to sound world-weary, and yet very educated:

'On broken wings
No bird can fly.'

At fourteen she was sent to work as a maid to an asylum in Roscommon for the wealthy, female mad. Signs of industry come to the village. Plunketts' lorries of sand and Hartons' lorries of gravel pull in to let each other by. I get a summer job, five shillings a day, delivering scrap and sheeps' fleeces to Athlone with Harry Ross, the jewman. He never eats more than an egg, but has a son a doctor in Dublin. When it rains and we cannot work, he still pays me. John Wilson TD, present Minister of Transport and Tourism, a Greek and Latin scholar, and mooted as future President of Ireland, lives on the Cavan side of the Bridge. Pollution is rampant. My first writings on the state of the lakes are rejected by the local paper. The Tidy Towns Committee have installed trees. My mother goes past in a cart to a dancing class in Togher. A man with a cure for the worms stands in the hall, and when later he touches your head, and mumbles his prayer, and you open your eyes, you feel you have been swimming underwater in some exalted place. He gets up on his bicycle and rides off, a timid man, with a passion for owls.

I knew it was time to go one day. A dusty afternoon saw Charlie Clavin deliver us into Cavan. It was of a Thursday, half-day in the town. The next day I asked for the Finea loaf. That was square bread all of a piece with a bronze hat and a crisp bottom. What they'd offered was the sliced pan. My father no longer wore a uniform, but stood up in the bakery shovelling coke into the furnace. Sundays he'd sit in the bakery with the newspapers. His lungs gave out. I sat at his bedside for two years with my books propped against his knees in the bed. My mother became a business lady. When they sent me into the convent I thought the nuns were wren boys. Cavan had a cinema. From then on my life divides into two halves. Most of the first part comes through the lips of my mother. At any hour we are back in Finea. She is old enough now to have settled there again, permanently, in the mind. So she'll die there at some moment in the past. Maybe on the day my father asked for her hand. She'd behind his back got engaged to a Guard McLoughlin. And meanwhile she had been courting Sonny Fitzgerald. Now one day her mother told her Guard Healy was at the door. Well, she took off the engagement ring and threw it onto the armchair opposite. Jack Healy – as these things will – came in and unknowingly sat on the ring and asked her to consider him.

In later life I made Sheelin into the Atlantic. Kinale, I've never got to the bottom of. It's got secrets that shouldn't be told. A time that can't be given back, but is, continuously. I always smoke a cigarette in the dark before sleeping, and all I've ever written about has a bridge, a man in uniform, a woman who takes the reins of a business. A girl at Loreto. In behind are the silent ones, my sisters, the brother. They too have their Finea, more complete than mine, being older. What happened is a wonder, though memory is always incomplete, like a map with a place missing. But it's all right, it's entered the imagination and nothing is ever the same. As for the rest of the county of Westmeath, it was, and remains, the great unknown. They've reared Grand National winners there. Hold cock-fights. Have hunts. I myself was married to a girl who came from that world and was brought up in the house where J. P. Donleavy now lives, outside Mullingar. My Mullingar is a place where first my Victorian grandfather, Thomas Slack, as an old RIC sergeant, walked to court, followed years after by my father, a Free-State guard, who went by bicycle. (Mullingar is also the place where on the street a veteran of World War II used to take two steps forward and one step backward, repeating, as he surveyed the garrison town, 'I'm walking knee-deep through the vermin of the Town Commissioners.') Athlone I returned to once with a theatre group called the Hacklers with a version of *Waiting for Godot*, which won the All-Ireland Drama Festival there. It was a great moment. I've passed the big houses and heard the rain drumming on the outhouses. Stood by the canal. It was a different world. Once I mitched from school and got kicked by an ass. I came to in a field where primroses were growing. That is the feeling.

And that's about it – except to mention that I often wonder how things would have gone if Sonny Fitzgerald had been my father. I'd like to be trying that out, maybe as a buttress against nostalgia that steals material from the same source as fiction, then leaves the reality wanting.

217 Nora and Maggie, Cork, Co. Cork

218 Three men, Cork, Co. Cork

COUNTY CORK

William Trevor

A personal truth hammers away whenever I'm in County Cork: here is where I belong. I am captivated, easily, by the hills of Tuscany, by Venice, and the English Cotswolds. Rome and New York are exhilarating, and whenever I sit in the sunshine at the café across from Bellinzona railway station I feel that death would come gently there. But whether I like it or not, Cork is home.

This spacious county is the most varied in Ireland. The lush farming land of neighbouring Limerick and Tipperary influences its northern boundaries. The Waterford coastline does not obediently change character when Waterford has finished with it. West Cork has been filched from Kerry.

Cork is its people and its stories, its towns, its woods, mountain and meadow, river and stream, the sea of its coast. Cork is the lilt of its place-names – Caherbarnagh, Kilmichael, Drimoleague, Castletownshend, Watergrasshill, Inchigeelagh. The earls of Desmond were of Cork, and the great McCarthys. Art O'Leary was murdered at Carriganimma for refusing to sell his horse as cheaply as the penal laws demanded. Michael Collins was shot at Beal na mBlath. St Finbarr is the patron saint.

My earliest memories are here, of sunshine and weeds in a garden in Mitchelstown, civic guards in the barracks next door. I did not know then that this unexceptional little town, half-asleep beneath the twin shadows of the Galtees and the Knockmeal-downs, was renowned only for its martyrs and the manufacture of processed cheese. I did not know that its limestone caves and passages attract a rare spider.

Today Mitchelstown is wide awake and doing nicely in all sorts of ways. So is Fermoy, directly to the south, a once-orderly garrison town, now a bustling shopping centre on the wide banks of the Blackwater. West of Fermoy, on that same river, is Mallow, with a hint or two remaining of its Georgian grandeur. The three towns form a triangle in North Cork, within and around which are the tree-studded meadows of great estates that must once have seemed impregnable. The Rakes of Mallow rampaged here, hunting and galloping and shouting their heads off. Edmund Spenser looked out from Kilcolman Castle and, line by line, advanced his *Faerie Queene*. Had my family remained in Mitchelstown I would have been one of the many small boys who were employed every summer to field the tennis-balls when they bounced out of court at the Bowenscourt tennis parties.

The rakes of Mallow belong in gardens now. A local poet writes, not of 'the vine-prop Elme, the Poplar neuer dry', but of the last train at Fermoy station, 1967. A bungalow has replaced Bowenscourt. Yet the truth that Ireland is nowhere successful in shaking off its several pasts is as evident in this part of County Cork as it is along its western or eastern borders.

I grew up in Youghal, where the Blackwater slips into the sea. It's a town no one could dislike, mildly fashionable as a watering-place in my childhood, with pierrots performing on the sands and old men painting garish, marvellous pictures with coloured powders. Beach pyjamas, sometimes garish also, were on parade from June to August, and once during the season the St Vincent de Paul trains brought the barefoot children from the back streets of the city for a day by the sea.

A time came when the promenade boarding-houses of Youghal lost their appeal, and with it their heart. Tattiness set in, looking as though it had come to stay. In fact it hadn't: it was just that change was on the way. The town is bigger now, its attractions different: seafood and discos, a good cup of coffee. The quays are cleaner, the fishermen fewer, the Devonshire Arms has had another lick of paint. But the view across the estuary has scarcely altered, nor has the squat little lighthouse. Myrtle Grove, where Sir Walter Raleigh lived, is wearing well; so is St Mary's Church, the Clock Tower, and the Loreto Convent where I learned to read and write.

There is a quality about East Cork, about the flat ordinariness that stretches inland from Ballycotton Bay, about the village of Cloyne and the town of Midleton, and the estuary landscape of Youghal, that gives the area its character. It is an unassuming quality, a lack of drama, and this is in the people also – the Ronans, the Allens, the Kierans, the Cotters, the Ormonds. Yew likes the local soil, in fact gave Youghal its name. The Vikings liked the undemanding terrain.

The town of Skibbereen, where next I lived, is now, in tourist-conscious Ireland, a cathedral city. It always was, of course, but in my time no one thought to mention it. More than eighty miles west of Youghal, through Cork city and untidy Bandon, through Clonakilty which people used to call Clonakilty-God-help-us, the journey to Skibbereen in the 1930s was a journey to the back of beyond.

The landscape is more ragged here. Gorse grows well. Speckled rock surfaces break out in the patchwork of fields. Once upon a time the countrywomen of West Cork wore strangely hooded black cloaks as they walked these roads and lanes, or sat in their donkey-butts. They greeted you from the shadowy depths, their singsong accent and easy laughter dispelling the suggestion of the sinister that this dress evoked. To this day, on a Sunday, their menfolk pitch heavy metal bowls along the same roads, laying wagers and marking with a sod torn from a ditch the length achieved by each. When a car appears they wave it on, but the tourists are a hazard now.

Skibbereen is famous because the *Skibbereen Eagle* once admonished Stalin, warning him that it had him in its sights. A grey figure still marks the town's centre, a statue of the Maid of Erin. The streets are narrow, the shops for the most part modest, the banks big, the pubs frequent: a good business town. I remember the source of that business: great cattle fairs, the gutters running with dung, palm striking palm as the bargain is struck, the purchased animals driven off after a few glassfuls have been raised. 'Place of the little boats': Skibbereen's river is the Ilen; the sea's just down the road.

The coastline becomes jagged, all bits and pieces and broken-off islands, bays within bays, slivers of peninsula. Turf bogs and hills, rocky land, marshy land, useless land, here and there an acre of grass: the Wild West of Cork begins beyond Ballydehob. A railway used to run by the roadside, with a once-a-day cow-catcher to the village of Skull.

Inland, to the right, St Finbarr built a church on an islet at Gougane Barra, the source of the River Lee, which meanders its way on to Cork itself. Here the disparate elements of the county merge. The natives speak swiftly in the city, but the country people keep their end up and are, in turn, never underestimated. This was the Mecca of my childhood, the metropolis that offered everything the small-town provincial could wish for.

No memory has remained as sharply etched as the escape to the paradise that was Cork city. Nothing has since out-dazzled the winter lights of Patrick Street or out-shrieked the cry of the evening paper-boys. Woolworth's was a wonder. In Lester's the girls had long bright fingernails and lipstick subtly applied, and weren't in the least like Mrs Hickey of Hickey's Medical Hall at home. The mirrored glass of the Victoria Hotel reflected a sophistication not readily to be found in Eldon's in Bridge Street; the Munster Arcade could have contained Power's drapery a dozen times over. No theatre has since cast such magic as the old Cork Opera House, *Babes in the Wood* on St Stephen's Day, *The White Horse Inn*.

In the cafés attached to the Savoy and the Pavilion the waitresses hurried with silver-plated teapots and silver-plated cake-stands. Bread was cut thinly and buttered; buns were brown or had currants; you eyed the pink icing of a cake. All around you there was steam and clatter and laughter, packets of Sweet Afton or Craven A thrown down casually on white table-cloths. Stylish women conversed, occasionally glancing about them, occasionally nodding a salutation through the crowd. The city's businessmen ordered bacon and kidneys, with an egg or a chop, and called out for Yorkshire Relish sauce. The glamour was the glamour of Carole Lombard, of *Fast and Loose* and *Too Hot to Handle*, of the cocktail world of Myrna Loy and William Powell. You wanted to stay there for ever.

The once-palatial picture-houses of Cork city aren't what they used to be. The great cafés – and the Victoria Hotel itself – have gone. But Father Mathew still advocates temperance from his pedestal, and sunlight sparkles on the waters of the Lee as ever it did. The wearying hills of Cork weary still, the Shandon bells haven't changed their tune. And what's true for the city's essence is true for the county's: from Mizen Head to Castletownroche, from Dungourney to Macroom, that thread of continuity persists in spite of the vicissitudes. It's there in the lakes of the Lee, and the banks of the Bandon, in Buttevant and Unionhall and Roaringwater Bay. It's there in the confidence and the guile, in the hint of cynicism behind easygoing eyes. It's there in the voice – the sound of Cork that time cannot touch.

222 Cork, Co. Cork

223 Christ among the chocolates, Cork, Co. Cork

224 Co. Cavan

COUNTY CAVAN

Tom MacIntyre

Cabhán – a hollow, a cave, a little hill, a deep wound . . .

Ireland's 'Drumlin Belt' – a thirty-mile-wide strip of hill and lake country – stretches east–west across the island from Down to Donegal. Cavan lies in the middle of it, veritable hinterland. The county divides into three parts: the Eastern Highlands, the Erne Valley, and the mountainy region of West Cavan.

The mountain nearest my home town in the Eastern Highlands is called Loughanlea – 'The Mountain of the Lake of the Cure'. I'd always been told that from its peaks you might glimpse the sea. A day came. I climbed, found the look-out point, and – some thirty miles eastward – saw sunlight imping on the Irish Sea.

The image haunted me. And out of the haunting rose a question. Didn't it follow that from the mountains of West Cavan you might catch the Atlantic? I would discover. In good time a climber sat opposite me. He was fresh from the Cuilcaghs, the West Cavan range where the Shannon rises.

'Can you see the Atlantic from up there?'

'Certainly.'

Through him, on the instant, I could chase the light on Donegal Bay.

Image, and answering image: in my deep breath I felt nurtured. Contentedly, I waited.

A dream came. I was in Cavan, talking to a group of people about the county. Those sea-glimpses, timbered fecundity of the valley between, the lakes past numbering . . . And, within the dream, to a dunt of exhilaration, I realised I was describing the curve of a life, the journey from sea to sea, dark and bright of the journey.

On the heels of that, another dream. I'm in Cavan again. Eating a tree. That was no *petit repas*.

Landscape

The eastern mountains
glimpse the sea,

and, climbers tell,
the western mountains
the greater sea,

the heartland plies
saucy shadow, secret
places, lakes
never yet found . . .

Sod of birth,
sod of death,

ask me again
to eat the tree.

227 Retreat, Co. Cavan

228 Cliff face, Co. Clare

COUNTY CLARE

Edna O'Brien

Just as countries have complexes, so do counties. Clare had no Lakes of Killarney or any big city with a statue of Lord Nelson or the emancipator Daniel O'Connell. Indeed, in Ennis, the capital, it was said that the streets were so narrow the people could shake hands from opposite windows. Severe and somewhat saintly, Eamonn De Valera was one TD and for the Opposition, a fluent man called Paddy Hogan who when asked by a heckler in Scariff, 'How many toes has a pig?' was said to have replied to his assailant, 'Take off your boots and count them.' I did not witness this exchange but heard it from my father. A story once told would be told again and again. Stories were the chief nourishment. We would go out at night to hear the wireless, in someone else's house, as one of the batteries – the wet one or the dry one – was banjaxed. I heard of the King's abdication, Chamberlain's speech and Amy Johnson's flight across the Atlantic on these crackling brown boxes, and all three events seemed of equal but baffling importance. In other words, the world outside was where things happened and we were not part of it. Yet we were endangered. According to a madman who had read the almanacs and had travelled, the end of the world was nigh. To give credibility to this a frog flew out of the ash-pit as the man had prophesied. At a wake. There were more wakes than weddings.

Nature prevailed. The trees around our house are what I remember most, trees in either fair weather or foul; bent, thwarted, lofty, capacious. Lanes and by-roads were clogged with hawthorn, elder and briar; there were forts dark as tombs where the cattle repaired. Along with pasture we had many bogs, some of them uncut, so that they looked primeval. I did not know what primeval meant but I could wander in these ancient bogs smothered with yellow waving grass. The used bogs had little stacks of cut turf, each person's firing for the winter. The bog-holes were full of brown-black squelchy water. The birds were not exactly melodious, more plaintive. The lakes, large and small, were of a particular dark slate colour and it was easy to believe the legend that cities or civilisations had vanished beneath them. There was, to all of it, a sort of supernatural pulse, as if pagan forces pervaded.

Then there were the everyday catastrophes. Foxes were the cause of my mother's more manifest heartbreaks. A clutch of chickens, usually canary-coloured, would be in the yard, screeching one minute and lying dead the next, like bits of rag. The fox had been. Mr Reynard. Always Mr, which in itself must have coloured one's considerations about the male sex. Many an elderly and even an old man asked one for a kiss and I have a clear recollection of saying to one of these queer loping gents, in a simulation of calm, 'I'm too young to kiss,' whilst inwardly cowering. Deserted roads were more awesome than others and the woods were a fright.

The men broke in horses or trained greyhounds and had terrible tempers. The women were mostly Veronicas. A neighbour of ours, a woman, would come from her lonely house away in the fields and yet, upon arrival, would announce that she couldn't stay a minute and that she must not come indoors. She refused everything, even buttermilk, and asked my mother if she had any news. News was some sort of elixir. News might change our lot, except that there was very little news, and our lot was more or less ordained. It is true that later on Shannon Airport was opened, but it is also true that on the first flight, when the pilot asked for guidance from the man in the control tower, he was solemnly told 'Repeat after me' and the man recited the Act of Perfect Contrition.

I am not presenting my county in a ridiculous light – far from it. I think they were a wild, unpredictable and highly-strung people. Though I had not read him then, the author I would come to regard as most cannily depicting County Clare was J. M. Synge. Christy Mahon was one of us. He was a blacksmith with eyes dancing in his head, hammering shoes and nailing them to the calloused soles of obstreperous horses. He claimed that John Ford had stopped him on a street in Limerick and had implored him to be a film star. Lies, or at least exaggeration, were essential to give a bit of spice to life.

Synge himself has said that if the Aran women had not worn the red petticoats that gave a splash of colour to the environment, then the people might have smashed their brains on the stones to create the necessary vividness. Our madness sustained us, or at least lifted us from the dross. An unpoetic poetry had its grip on us. Curses too. Dark fluent spells deep as the lakes. There was nothing pretty unless it be the primroses. The dogs were riotous. Shades of the witch with her black bottle crept into conversation, the pagan witch versus the hierarchy. Crowning the hotch-potch of half-baked mythology was the wrenching story of Colleen Bawn, drowned by a wicked suitor; the steel of her corset however, the incriminating evidence, washed up on the Shannon estuary.

Our own house of course was the centre of my universe. Big rooms, silent spheres with ornaments and, as I believed, spirits. I had not read Proust then, but the church steeple, the hawthorn bushes, the clotted velvet roses on the chenille cloth and the by-roads that led to nowhere made me want to write about them as if their existence was incomplete, otherwise. My own existence too. Writing stems from an acute longing and a malcontent. Clare, with its songs, its wildness and its purple gloom, was the ideal cradle for that perverse profession. You may ask why I write about the Clare of then rather than of now. The answer is simple. The then is what formed me and, as W. B. Yeats has said, 'Friendship never ends.' Neither do one's first affiliations.

231 The wastes, The Burren, Co. Clare

232 High ground, The Burren, Co. Clare

233 After the storm, The Burren, Co. Clare

JOHN BANVILLE was born in Wexford in 1945. His novels include *Birchwood* (1973), *Doctor Copernicus*, which won the James Tait Black Memorial Prize in 1976, *Kepler*, which was awarded the Guardian Fiction Prize in 1981, *The Newton Letter* (1982), *Mefisto* (1986) and *The Book of Evidence* (1989). John Banville is literary editor of the *Irish Times* and lives in Dublin with his wife and two sons.

EMMA COOKE was born in Co. Offaly in 1934. She has published many short stories in magazines and on radio. In 1988 her story *An International Incident* was awarded second place in the Francis McManus Radio Short Story competition. Her books are *Female Forms* (1980), *A Single Sensation* (1981) and *Eve's Apple* (1985). She lives in Killaloe, Co. Clare.

ANNE DEVLIN was born in Belfast in 1951 and now lives in Birmingham with her husband and son. She teaches a Playwriting Course at Birmingham University, and has written for radio, television and the stage and published a collection of short stories. Her awards include the Samuel Beckett Award for the Best First Play for Television (1985), and the George Devine Award (Jt) for her play *Ourselves Alone* (1986).

EILÍS DILLON was born in Galway and spoke Gaelic from childhood. Widowed in 1970, she is now married to the author and critic Vivian Mercier. Best known as a novelist and author of children's fiction, she is also a poet and playwright. Her most recent novels are *Citizen Burke* and *The Interloper*. She is a member of Aosdána and a Fellow of the Royal Society of Literature.

CHRISTOPHER FITZ-SIMON was born in Belfast. He works in the theatre and broadcasting, and has lectured on Irish drama and related subjects around the world. His chief publications are *The Arts in Ireland* (1982) and *The Irish Theatre* (1983); he has also written short stories and radio plays. He has held appointments as Artistic Director of the Irish Theatre Company and the National Theatre Society (Abbey and Peacock Theatres) and is a founder-director of Siamsa Tire and of the Tyrone Guthrie Centre.

MICHAEL HARTNETT was born in Co. Limerick in 1941. He writes poetry in both Irish and English and translates from Spanish. He has published over twenty collections, the most recent being *Poems to Younger Women* (1988). He lectures at home, in the UK, Europe and the USA. He lives in Dublin.

DERMOT HEALY was born in Finea, Co. Westmeath, in 1947 and now lives at Rosses Point, Co. Sligo. His books are *Banished Misfortune* (stories) and *Fighting with Shadows* (novel); his plays are *The Long Swim*, *Curtains* and a translation of Lorca's *Blood Wedding*. He has also written a film script, *Our Boys*. He is the editor of the magazine *The Drumlin*, and is a member of Aosdána.

SEAMUS HEANEY was born near Castledawson in Co. Derry in 1939. He has published seven collections of poetry including *Death of a Naturalist* (1966), *North* (1975), *Field Work* (1979) and *The Haw Lantern* (1987), two volumes of criticism and a translation of the Irish poem *Buile Suibhne*. He now lives in Dublin.

AIDAN HIGGINS was born in 1927 in Celbridge, Co. Kildare. His books include the novels *Langrishe, Go Down* (1966), which won the James Tait Black Memorial Prize and the Irish Academy of Letters Award and was filmed for television with a screenplay by Harold Pinter, and *Balcony of Europe* (1972), which was shortlisted for the Booker Prize. His selected travel writing, *Ronda Gorge and Other Precipices*, and selected stories, *Helsingør Station and Other Departures*, were published this year.

DESMOND HOGAN was born in Ballinasloe, Co. Galway, in 1951. His novels and collections of stories include *The Mourning Thief*, *Lebanon Lodge*, *A New Shirt* and *A Curious Street*. *A Link with the River* — his complete short stories — was published recently in America.

NEIL JORDAN was born in Sligo in 1950. He is the author of *Night in Tunisia and Other Stories* (1976), which won the Guardian Fiction Prize, *The Past* (1979) and *The Dream of a Beast* (1983). Best known as an award-winning film-maker, he wrote and directed *Angel* (1982), and directed *Company of Wolves* (1984), *Mona Lisa* (1986) and *High Spirits* (1988).

MAEVE KELLY grew up in Dundalk; she left it in 1951 to begin a nursing career in London. She married in 1958 and she and her husband farmed in Co. Clare. She now lives near Limerick. Her books are *A Life of Her Own* (stories, 1976), *Necessary Treasons* (novel, 1985), *Resolution* (poems, 1986) and *Florrie's Girls* (novel, 1989).

BRENDAN KENNELLY was born in Ballylongford, Co. Kerry, in 1936. He has written many collections of verse, and two novels. His play *Medea* was awarded the Irish Critics' Special Harvey's Award. He is the editor of *The Penguin Book of Irish Verse* and *Landmarks of Irish Drama*, and Professor of Modern Literature at Trinity College, Dublin.

BENEDICT KIELY was born in Dromore, Co. Tyrone, in 1919, and worked as a journalist in Dublin from 1940 to 1965. He has written numerous novels — including

Proxopera (1977) and *Nothing Happens in Carmincross* (1985) — works of non-fiction and short-story collections, his latest being *A Letter to Peachtree* (1987). He is editor of the *Penguin Book of Irish Short Stories*. His awards include the Irish Academy of Letters Award (1980).

THOMAS KILROY's novel *The Big Chapel* was set in his native County Kilkenny. It won the Guardian Fiction Prize and was shortlisted for the 1971 Booker Prize. His stage plays include *The Death and Resurrection of Mr Roche*, *Talbot's Box* and *Double Cross*. He made a successful adaptation of Chekhov's *The Seagull* and has recently adapted Ibsen's *Ghosts*. He is a Fellow of the Royal Society of Literature, a member of the Irish Academy of Letters and a director of Field Day Theatre Company.

MICHAEL LONGLEY was born in Belfast in 1939. His poetry collections are *No Continuing City* (1969), *An Exploded View* (1976), *Man Lying on a Wall* (1976), *The Echo Gate* (1979) and, in 1985, *Poems 1963–1983*. He is married to the critic Edna Longley and they have three children. He works in Belfast as the Combined Arts Director of the Arts Council of Northern Ireland.

EUGENE McCABE was born in Glasgow in 1930. He is married to Margot Bowen and they have four children. He farmed intensively until 1966, when he began writing full-time. In 1964 his play *King of the Castle* won the Irish Life Award. His works have won Irish, English and international awards.

JOHN McGAHERN was born in 1934. His books include *The Barracks* (1963), *The Dark* (1965), *Nightlines* (1971), *The Pornographer* (1979) and *High Ground* (1985). His new novel will be published next year. He lives on a farm in County Leitrim.

MEDBH McGUCKIAN was born in Belfast in 1950, where she still lives. She has worked as an English teacher, and was writer-in-residence at Queen's University from 1986 to 1988. She is currently literary editor of a local magazine, *Fortnight*. Her books are *The Flower Master* (1982), *Venus and the Rain* (1984) and *On Ballycastle Beach* (1988).

FRANK McGUINNESS is a playwright and lives in Dublin. His work includes *The Factory Girls*, *Observe the Sons of Ulster Marching Towards the Somme*, *Baglady*, *Carthaginians* and *Mary and Lizzie*. His films include *Scout* and *The Hen House*.

TOM Mac INTYRE was born in Co. Cavan and lives in Dublin. He has written fiction, poetry and drama. His most recent publications are *The Harper's Turn* (stories, 1982) and *I Baled Out at Ardee* (poems and translations, 1987). Of his theatre work, he is best known for *The Great Hunger*, based on Patrick Kavanagh's poem.

AIDAN MATHEWS was born in 1956 in Dublin. His published work includes two selections of poetry, *Windfalls* (1976) and *Minding Ruth* (1983); three plays: *The Diamond Body*, *The Antigone* and *Exit/Entrance*; and a collection of stories, *Adventures in a Bathyscope* (1988). He has received several prizes, including the Irish Times Award in 1974, the Patrick Kavanagh Award in 1976, the Macauley Fellowship in 1978–9 and an Academy of American Poets Award in 1982. He lives near Dublin with his wife and daughter.

BRIAN MOORE was born in Belfast in 1921. He emigrated to Canada in 1948, and moved to the United States in 1959 as a Guggenheim Fellow. He was Professor of English at UCLA from 1973 to 1988. His novels include *The Lonely Passion of Judith Hearne* (1955), *The Temptation of Eileen Hughes* (1981) and *The Colour of Blood* (1987). He has twice been shortlisted for the Booker Prize and has won a number of major literary awards, including the Sunday Express Book of the Year in 1986.

PAUL MULDOON was born in Co. Armagh in 1951. He now lives in the United States. His main collections of poetry are *New Weather* (1973), *Mules* (1977), *Why Brownlee Left* (1980), *Quoof* (1983), *Meeting the British* (1987) and *Selected Poems 1968–1983* (1986).

NUALA Ní DHOMHNAILL was born in St Helens, Lancashire, in 1952, and fostered in West Kerry. She is a full-time writer in Irish and is a frequent broadcaster with Radio na Gaeltachta, RTÉ and BBC Northern Ireland. She has published three books: *An Dealg Droighin* (1981), *Féar Suaithinseach* (1984) and *Rogha Dánta/Selected Poems* (1988), and two children's plays, *Jimín* and *An Ollphiast Ghránna*. She lives in Dublin with her husband and four children.

EDNA O'BRIEN is a native of Co. Clare and many of her works reflect that landscape. Her novels include *The Country Girls Trilogy*, *Night* and *A Pagan Place*; her collected stories are published under the title *A Fanatic Heart*. Her plays include *Virginia*, based on the life of Virginia Woolf. Her first volume of poetry, *On the Bone*, was published this year. She lives in London.

FRANK ORMSBY was born in Enniskillen in 1947. He is head of English at the Royal Belfast Adademical Institution. He has edited a number of anthologies and his two poetry collections, *A Store of Candles* (1977) and *A Northern Spring* (1986), were both Poetry Book Society choices.

JAMES PLUNKETT was born in Dublin in 1920. He worked as a trade union secretary and subsequently joined the staff of Radio Éireann, later transferring to television. His written work includes *The Eagles and the Trumpets* (1954), *The Trusting and the Maimed*

(1955), *Strumpet City* (1969), *Farewell Companions* (1977), *The Gems She Wore* (1978), *The Boy in the Wall* (1987) and the play *The Risen People*.

PETER SIRR was born in Waterford in 1960. In 1982 he won the Patrick Kavanagh Award and in 1985 and 1988 received bursaries in writing from the Irish Arts Council. His first collection of poems, *Marginal Zones*, was published in 1984, and *Talk, Talk* in 1987. He is one of the editors of *Graph*, the Irish critical magazine. He lives in Holland.

FRANCIS STUART was born in Australia in 1902 of Ulster parents, and fought in the Irish Civil War on the Republican side. He was married to Maud Gonne's daughter Iseult and has worked as a university lecturer and a broadcaster. Hailed by Yeats as one of the great new Irish writers, he has written poetry, plays and a number of novels, the best known of which are *The Pillar of Cloud* (1948), *Redemption* (1949) and *Black List, Section H* (1971). He lives in Dublin.

WILLIAM TREVOR was born in Mitchelstown, Co. Cork, in 1928. He is a member of the Irish Academy of Letters. He has written numerous books, including *The Old Boys* (1964), which was awarded the Hawthornden Prize; *The Ballroom of Romance* (1972); *Angels at the Ritz* (1975); *The Children of Dynmouth* (1976) and *Fools of Fortune* (1983), which won the Whitbread Best Novel Award. He has also written many plays for stage, radio and television, and many short stories. In 1976 he received the Allied Irish Banks' Prize and in 1977 was awarded an honorary CBE.

SEAN J. WHITE has been Dean of the School of Irish Studies in Dublin since 1980. A well known writer and broadcaster and a former editor of *Irish Writing* and *Poetry Ireland*, he is currently a Trustee of the James Joyce Foundation and Secretary of the Irish Academy of Letters.

Acknowledgements

My greatest thanks to Robin Robertson, for believing in me;
J. (F.) Ferguson, for being a friend; Norman Sivor, for the inspiration

The publisher wishes to express grateful acknowledgement to the following for permission to quote from published material:
Mrs Katherine B. Kavanagh, c/o Peter Fallon, Oldcastle, Co. Meath for 'Come Dance with Kitty Stobling' by Patrick Kavanagh (p. 62); James Brodie Ltd for 'The Deserted Village' by Oliver Goldsmith (p. 83); the Estate of Padraic Colum and Mrs Máire Colum O'Sullivan for *The King of Ireland's Son* by Padraic Colum (p. 85); the Mercier Press for *The Great Tyrconnel* by Charles Petrie (p. 90); the Dublin Institute for Advanced Studies for Cecile O'Rahilly's translation of *Táin Bó Cuailnge* (p. 101); the Irish Academic Press for *Love Songs of Connacht* by Douglas Hyde (p. 107); Faber & Faber Ltd and Farrar, Straus and Giroux, Inc. for 'Peninsula' from *Door into the Dark* by Seamus Heaney (p. 109); Faber & Faber Ltd and Doubleday, a division of Bantam, Doubleday, Dell Publishing Group, Inc. for 'The Far Field' (p. 139), copyright © 1962 by Beatrice Roethke, Administratrix of the Estate of Theodore Roethke, from *The Collected Poems of Theodore Roethke*; Macmillan, London and Basingstoke for 'Red Roses For Me' from *Three More Plays* by Sean O'Casey (p. 179), and for *Autobiographies* by Sean O'Casey (p. 179); Faber & Faber Ltd for 'Dublin' from *The Collected Poems of Louis MacNeice* (p. 180); Faber & Faber Ltd and Farrar, Straus and Giroux, Inc. for 'To The Sea' from *High Windows* by Philip Larkin (p. 199).

First published in Great Britain by
Martin Secker & Warburg Limited
Michelin House, 81 Fulham Road
London SW3 6RB

Copyright © 1989
Photographs © Donovan Wylie 1989
Text © the individual contributors 1989

Edited by Robin Robertson, Mark Holborn and Donovan Wylie
Designed by Chris Shamwana and Angus Hyland

A CIP catalogue record for this book is available from the British Library

ISBN 0 436 10254 4 (trade edition)
ISBN 0 436 10256 0 (limited edition)

Printed and bound in Great Britain by
Butler & Tanner Ltd, Frome, Somerset